THE STRASBURG MANUSCRIPT

DAS STRASSBURGER MANUSKRIPT

DAS STRASSBURGER MANUSKRIPT

Handbuch für Maler des Mittelalters

ENGLISCHE ÜBERSETZUNG AUS DEM MITTELHOCHDEUTSCHEN

VON

VIOLA & ROSAMUND BORRADAILE

DEUTSCHE ÜBERSETZUNG DES TEXTES DER HERAUSGEBER

VON JOHANNA M. FRANCK

VORWORT VON

JOHN HARTHAN
LEITER DER BIBLIOTHEK DES
VICTORIA & ALBERT MUSEUM, LONDON

NEW YORK / TRANSATLANTIC ARTS / 1966

THE STRASBURG MANUSCRIPT

A Medieval Painters' Handbook

TRANSLATED FROM THE OLD GERMAN

BY

VIOLA & ROSAMUND BORRADAILE

EDITORS' TEXT TRANSLATED INTO GERMAN

BY JOHANNA M. FRANCK

FOREWORD BY

JOHN HARTHAN
KEEPER OF THE LIBRARY OF THE
VICTORIA & ALBERT MUSEUM

NEW YORK / TRANSATLANTIC ARTS / 1966

We are indebted to Dr. Ph. Dollinger, Director of Les Archives et la Bibliothèque de la Ville de Strasbourg for supplying a transcript of the catalogue entry of the Strasburg Manuscript in the year 1846, which reads as under:

Wir sind ausserdem Herrn Dr. Ph. Dollinger, Direktor des Archives und der Bibliothèque de la Ville de Strasbourg, zu Dank verpflichtet für die Abschrift der Katalog-Eintragung des Strassburger Manuskripts im Jahre 1846, welche folgendermaassen lautet:

f ° 155a Das ist von Varwen (Farben), die mich lert meister Heinrich von Lübegge "Wiltu Lazur machen"

f ° 157a Dis lert mich Meister Andres von Kolmar "So du wilt einen grund machen"

f ° 181b "So wirt das Horn weich"

> 4°, papier, XVe siecle, écriture allemande moyenne, régulière, ligne longue

ND
1130
S813

FIRST AMERICAN EDITION:
TRANSATLANTIC ARTS INC.
565 FIFTH AVENUE
NEW YORK, NY 10017

52417

PRINTED BY LAWRENCE BROS. (Weston-super-Mare) LTD., WESTON-SUPER-MARE
BOUND BY C. & H. T. EVANS LTD., CROYDON

© ALEC TIRANTI LTD., LONDON W1
MADE AND PRINTED IN THE UNITED KINGDOM

CONTENTS

Acknowledgements 3

Foreword 5

Translators' Introduction 9

THE STRASBURG MANUSCRIPT 21

APPENDIX 75

Notes 89

Bibliography 112

Index 113

INHALT

Anerkennungen 2

Vorwort 4

Einleitung der Übersetzer 8

DAS STRASSBURGER MANUSKRIPT 20

ANHUNG 74

Anmerkungen 88

Literatur 112

Index 113

ANERKENNUNGEN

DIE ÜBERSETZER schulden den Trustees der National Gallery, London, für die gütige Erlaubnis, das Strassburger Manuskript zu veröffentlichen, grossen Dank, und ebenfalls Herrn Alec Tiranti für seinen Ünternehmungsgeist, die Veröffentlichung dieses Werkes zu übernehmen. Die Übersetzer möchten ausserdem Herrn John Harthan, dem Leiter der Bibliothek des Victoria und Albert Museums, ihre tiefgefühlte Dankbarkeit für seine Bereitschaft aussprechen, das Vorwort für diese Übersetzung zu schreiben und für zugleich die wertvollen Ratschläge, die er ihnen für eine Anzahl von Problemen, die in Verbindung mit dieser Arbeit auftauchten, gegeben hat. Sie möchten auch noch herzlichst all den hier angeführten Persönlichkeiten danken, die den Verfassern während der Arbeit an diesem Buch grosszügige Hilfe und Ermutigung gegeben haben:

Dame Marjorie Maxse

Miss Dorothy Hutton

Miss Joyce Plesters of the National Gallery (Scientific Dept.)

Miss Marianne Winders, formerly of the Institute of Germanic Literature and Languages

The Rev. A. R. Batchelor Wylam, Secretary of the Norfolk Advisory Committee for the Care of the Churches

Mrs. K. Thomson of the Records Office

Mrs. L. Sawyer and her daughter Jennifer

Miss P. I. Edwards of the Natural History Museum

Besonderen Dank schulden die Übersetzer Herrn Dr. Edmund Launert, Britiches Museum (Natural History Dept.), dafür, die deutschen Manuskript vorkommen, ausfindig gemacht zu haben.

Und schliesslich möchten die Autoren ausdrücken, welch grossen Dank sie jenen frühen Mitgliedern der Tempera Society schulden, die durch ihre Forschungen auf dem Gebiet der Maltechnik der Vergangenheit und durch ihre zahlreichen einschlägigen Experimente zum Verständnis dieses Manuskriptes beigetragen und damit eine klare Darstellung seines Inhaltes ermöglicht haben.

VIOLA UND ROSAMUND BORRADAILE

2

ACKNOWLEDGMENTS

THE THANKS of the translators are due to the Trustees of the National Gallery for their kind permission to publish the Strasburg Manuscript, as also to Mr. Alec Tiranti for his enterprise in undertaking the publication of this work. The writers also wish to express their deep sense of appreciation to Mr. John Harthan, Keeper of the Library of the Victoria and Albert Museum for his kindness in writing the Foreword to this translation and also for the valuable advice he has given on various matters connected with the work. Again they desire to offer their warm thanks to the following who have generously given help and encouragement to the writers throughout the preparation of this volume:

to Dame Marjorie Maxse
    Miss Dorothy Hutton
    Miss Joyce Plesters of the National Gallery (Scientific Dept.)
    Miss Marianne Winders, formerly of the Institute of Germanic
        Literature and Languages
    The Rev. A. R. Batchelor Wylam, Secretary of the Norfolk
        Advisory Committee for the Care of Churches
    Mrs. K. Thompson of the Records Office
    Mrs. L. Sawyer and her daughter Jennifer
    Miss P. I. Edwards of the Natural History Museum.

The translators' grateful acknowledgments are also specially due to Dr. Edmund Launert of the British Museum (Natural History Dept.), for tracking down the meaning of certain obscure botanical terms occurring in the German script.

Finally, the writers desire to record the magnitude of their debt to those early members of the Tempera Society who, by their researches into the painting techniques of the past and by their manifold experiments in this field, have contributed to the understanding of this manuscript and thus made possible an intelligible presentation of its contents.

VIOLA AND ROSAMUND BORRADAILE

VORWORT

DAS STRASSBURGER MANUSKRIPT, das älteste noch existierende deutsche Handbuch für die Maltechnik — es stammt wahrscheinlich aus dem 15. Jahrhundert, — ist bisher nur einigen Fachleuten in einer unvollständigen Übersetzung bekannt gewesen; sie war in Charles Eastlake's *Materials for a History of Oil Painting* (London 1847) enthalten. Eastlake's Übersetzung stammte von einer Abschrift des Original-Manuskriptes, die sich jetzt in der National Gallery, London, befindet. Ohne diese wäre wahrscheinlich jede Kenntnis dieses einzigartigen mittelalterlichen Malerhandbuches für unsere Zeit verloren gegangen; denn das Manuskript selbst wurde durch das katastrophale Feuer in der Strassburger Stadtbibliothek im Jahre 1870 zerstört. Im Jahre 1897 veröffentlichte der deutsche Gelehrte Ernst Berger eine kitische Ausgabe des Textes mit Kommentar in *Beiträge zur Entwicklungsgeschichte der Maltechnik*, (Band 3, Seiten 148–176;), aber bis zum heutigen Tage existiert weder eine vollständige englische Übersetzung noch eine systematische Untersuchung des Dokumentes.

Diesem Mangel ist nun durch die Übersetzung von Eastlake's wertvoller Übertragung durch Viola und Rosamund Borradaile abgeholfen worden. Da beide ausübende Künstler un Restauratoren von Kirchendenkmälern sind, steht ihnen eine Fülle von technischem Wissen und von Erfahrung zur Verfügung, die sie instandsetzte, die ausserordentliche Aufgabe zu bewältigen, deutschen Dialekt des 15. Jahrhunderts in modernes Englisch zu übertragen. Diese genaue und urkundlich belegte Kenntnis von Rezepten und Verfahren, die man in spätmittelalterlichen Ateliers anwendete, gibt nicht nur über die Herstellung von Gemälden und Buch-Illuminierungen Auskunft, sie gibt auch modernen Bildrestauratoren wertvolle Anleitunen. Die Untersuchung ist ausserdem von grosser Bedeutung für die sehr aktuellen Probleme des Reinigens alter Bilder.

Es muss den beruflichen Kunsthistorikern überlassen bleiben, die Bedeutung des Strassburger Manuskriptes für die Entwicklung spätmittelalterlicher Malerei und Illuminierung zu bewerten.

Im vorliegenden Werk haben sich die Übersetzer in erster Linie darum bemüht, einen grundlegenden englischen Text zu schaffen, und in ihren Anmerkungen die Bedeutung unbekannter Ausdrücke

4

FOREWORD

THE STRASBURG MANUSCRIPT, the oldest surviving manual on painting techniques in the German language and dating probably from the fifteenth century, has hitherto been known only to specialists in an incomplete translation incorporated by Sir Charles Eastlake into his *Materials for a History of Oil Painting* (London 1847). Eastlake's translation was made from a transcript of the original manuscript, now in the National Gallery, London, without which it is probable that today all knowledge of this unique medieval painters' handbook would be lost, for the Manuscript itself perished in the disastrous fire of 1870 in the Strasburg City Library. In 1897 the German scholar Ernst Berger published a critical edition of the text (with commentary) in his *Beiträge zur Entwicklungsgeschichte der Maltechnik* (Vol. 3, pp. 148–176), but there has hitherto been no complete English translation nor systematic study of the document.

This want is now supplied by the translation which Viola and Rosamund Borradaile have prepared from Eastlake's precious transcript. As practising artists and church monument restorers they have been able to draw on a joint fund of technical knowledge and experience in tackling the difficult task of rendering fifteenth century German dialect into accurate, modern English. Such precise, documented knowledge of the recipes and procedures followed in late medieval workshops not only provides information about how paintings and manuscript illuminations were actually produced, but gives valuable guidance to restorers today. It is also highly relevant to the current controversy concerning the cleaning of old pictures.

Assessment of the significance of the Strasburg Manuscript in the development of late medieval painting and illumination must await the attention of professional art historians. In the present work the translators are primarily concerned with establishing a standard English text and with patiently investigating, in the Notes, the meaning of obscure terms and doubtful passages. It is good to know that such valuable source material as the Strasburg Manuscript will now be readily available to students of medieval painting. It is also salutary sometimes to remember that art history is not exclusively

und anzweifelbarer Textstellen mit Geduld zu untersuchen. Es ist sehr erfreulich, dass solch wertvolles Quellenmaterial wie das Strassburger Manuskript von jetzt an allen zugänglich sein wird, die mittelalterliche Malerei studieren. Vielleicht ist es auch von Wert, sich gelegentlich daran zu erinnern, dass Kunstgeschichte nicht ausschliesslich eine Sache von Stil und Technik ist, sondern dass sie auch die Entwicklung der Technik und die Wiederentdeckung der einst so sorgsam gehüteten Geheimnisse einer verschwundenen Tradition mitumfasst.

JOHN HARTHAN

NACHWORT DES DEUTSCHEN VERLEGERS

Im Vorwort wie im Text wird des öfteren auf Ernst Bergers *Beiträge zur Entwicklungsgeschichte der Maltechnik* verwiesen. Die dritte Folge des Werkes erschien 1897. Eine zweite, durchgesehene Auflage erschien 1912. Da diese wertvollen, im Verlag Callwey erschienenen Arbeiten, die auch das Strassburger Manuskript enthielten, längst vergriffen sind, hat der Verlag Callwey gern die deutsche Ausgabe der verdienstvollen englischen Veröffentlichung übernommen.

Karl Baur-Callwey

a matter of styles and techniques but comprises as well the development of techniques and rediscovery of the once closely guarded secrets of a vanished tradition.

JOHN HARTHAN

EINLEITUNG DER ÜBERSETZER

ZAHLLOSE BESUCHER strömen jahrein, jahraus in die National Gallery, um sich an der grossartigen Sammlung der dort ausgestellten Bilder zu erfreuen. Wenige, oder vielleicht keiner dieser Besucher, haben jedoch jemals von einem ganz andersartigen Schatz gehört, der unter demselben Dach gehütet wird, — dem Strassburger Manuskript. Dieses Dokument ist, trotzdem es nur klein und unbedeutend aussieht, ein unschätzbarer Bericht über Malmethoden und Malmaterialien, der uns aus dem Mittelalter überliefert worden ist.

Dieses deutsche Manuskript ist seit einiger Zeit von Fachleuten als eines der bedeutendsten Dokumente über frühe Malmethoden anerkannt worden. Man mag es tatsächlich in mancher Hinsicht mit Cennini's *Trattato* vergleichen, obgleich zugegeben werden muss, dass es nicht so umfassend ist wie jene berühmte Arbeit.

Ernst Berger, die hervorragende deutsche Autorität auf dem Gebiet der Maltechniken und ihrer Geschichte, ist der Ansicht, das Strassburger Manuskript sei im 15. Jahrhundert enstanden, während Sir Charles Eastlake (1793–1865) es in eine Zeit nicht später als das erste Viertel des 14. Jahrhunderts verweist. In welchem dieser beiden Jahrhunderte es auch entstanden sein mag, so ist seine Bedeutung als Zeugnis für die in den alten Werkstätten Nordeuropas ausgeübten Malmethoden unbestreitbar.

Eastlake war der erste, der wenigstens Teile dieses wertvollen Dokumentes ins Englische übersetzte und der Auszüge davon in sein Werk *Materials for a History of Oil Painting*, (veröffentlicht im Jahre 1847) aufnahm. Diese Abhandlung wird unsern Lesern zweifellos bekannt sein. Während Eastlake mit der Zusammenstellung dieser Arbeit beschäftigt war, gelang es ihm, durch die gütige Hilfe von Herrn Lewis Gruner, eine Abschrift des Strassburger Manuskriptes von der Strassburger Bibliothek zu erhalten. Wie es sich später herausstellte, war es ein grosses Glück, dass diese Abschrift überhaupt gemacht worden war, denn im Jahre 1870 wurde die Strassburger Bibliothek, in der sich das Manuskript befand, durch Feuer zerstört, und das Original ging für immer verloren.

Die für Eastlake hergestellte Abschrift, die sich jetzt in der Bibliothek der National Gallery in London befindet, und die die einzige bekannte ist, die direkt vom Original gemacht wurde (gemäss

8

TRANSLATORS' INTRODUCTION

COUNTLESS VISITORS stream through the National Gallery year by year, to enjoy the magnificent collection of paintings there on view. Few if any of these visitors, however, have so much as heard of a treasure of quite another kind housed under the same roof—the Strasburg Manuscript. This document although in itself both small and insignificant looking constitutes a precious record of painters' methods and materials which has come down to us from medieval times.

This German Manuscript has, for some time, been recognised by experts as one of the most outstanding documents relating to early painting methods. It may indeed be compared in some respects with Cennini's *Trattato*, although admittedly less comprehensive in scope than that famous work.

According to Ernst Berger, the eminent German authority on painting techniques and their history, the Strasburg Manuscript belongs to the fifteenth century, while Sir Charles Eastlake (1793–1865) assigned it to a period not later than the first quarter of the fourteenth. To whichever of these two centuries it belongs however, its importance as documentary evidence concerning the early workshop practice of painters in Northern Europe is incontestable.

Eastlake was the first to translate any part of this valuable document into English and introduced extracts from it in his *Materials for a History of Oil Painting* (published 1847), with which treatise readers will doubtless be familiar. It was whilst compiling this work that Eastlake succeeded in obtaining a copy of the Manuscript in question from the Library at Strasburg, through the kind offices of Mr. Lewis Gruner. As subsequent events proved, it was indeed fortunate that this copy had been made, for in the year 1870, the Strasburg Library, where the Manuscript was lodged, was destroyed by fire and the original document lost for ever.

The transcript made for Eastlake, now in the National Gallery Library, being the only one known to have been taken directly from the original (listed as MS. A VI 19 according to Prof. D. V. Thompson), is therefore of an importance not to be underestimated. Some sixty years ago, in his *Beiträge*, Ernst Berger published the greater part of the text, accompanied by an extensive commentary. Until now,

9

Herrn Professor D. V. Thompson als M.S.A.VI.19 verzeichnet), ist daher von nicht zu unterschätzender Bedeutung. Ernst Berger veröffentlichte den grösseren Teil des Textes, der von einem ausführlichen Kommentar begleitet war, vor etwa 60 Jahren in seinen *Beiträgen*. Jedoch ist bis zum heutigen Tage keine englische Version des Gesamt-Manuskriptes erschienen. Der Grund hierfür mag in den störenden Wirkungen zweier Weltkriege liegen, die den freien Gedankenaustausch zwischen Gelehrten verschiedener Länder leider unterbrachen. Ein Dokument, dessen Inhalt von solch vitalem Interesse für Künstler und Kunsthistoriker ist, wäre unter günstigeren Umständen sicherlich nicht so lange vernachlässigt worden.

Das Manuskript wurde in der Sprachweise, die als Mittel-Hochdeutsch bekannt ist, niedergeschrieben. Seine Übersetzung ins Englische ist keineswegs eine einfache Aufgabe gewesen. Die Schwierigkeiten lagen nicht nur in der Sprache selbst und im Fehlen der Interpunktion, sondern auch in dem Bruch in der Tradition des eigentlichen Malverfahrens. Die Ausdeutung des Inhaltes wäre tatsächlich fast unmöglich gewesen, wenn die Übersetzer nicht bereits selbst gewisse Kenntnisse der im Text beschriebenen Arbeitsmethoden besessen hätten; wie z.B. der Herstellung von Pergamentleimen, von Ölen und Firnissen, dem Reiben von Farbstoffen und den dazugehörigen Bindemitteln, und dazu noch anderer Arbeitsverfahren, die obgleich sie in der Vergangenheit einen Teil der täglichen Arbeitsroutine bildenten, heute nicht mehr zur Ausbildung des Künstlers gehören. Es wird sich daher zeigen, dass die Erfahrungen, die beim tatsächlichen Arbeiten mit den im Manuskript behandelten Substanzen gemacht wurden, und die Beobachtungen ihrer Reaktionen unter wechselnden Bedingungen, zum Verständnis von vielem, das sonst wohl unverständlich geblieben wäre, beigetragen haben. Zusätzlich wäre zu sagen, dass diese Kenntnisse der Arbeitsverfahren es möglich gemacht haben, einige der kleinen Schreibfehler, die immer in derartigen Dokumenten hier und da auftauchen, und die manchmal zu Missverständnissen beim Lesen führen, richtig zu stellen.

In den letzten Jahren sind viele Neuauflagen und Übersetzungen alter Mal-Manuale im Druck erschienen. Solche Veröffentlichungen werden meistens als gelehrte Untersuchungen sehr begrüsst. Sie werden auch als bedeutsam vom historischen Gesichtspunkt ausbetrachtet. Doch nur selten, wenn überhaupt, mit Ausnahme von Cennini's *Trattato*, sind sie von Wichtigkeit für die Arbeitsweisen, die heutzutage von Künstlern ausgeübt werden. Und dennoch enthalten diese alten Berichte ein Fülle von Wissenswertem, das

however, no English version of the Manuscript as a whole has appeared. This is probably due to the disruptive effects of two world wars, during which the free exchange of ideas between scholars of different countries was of necessity interrupted. Under more favourable conditions a document containing matter of such interest to artists and art historians is unlikely to have been neglected for so long.

The Manuscript is written in the dialect known as Old Middle German. Its translation into English has been by no means an easy task, not only by reason of the difficulties presented by the language, and the lack of punctuation, but also on account of the break with tradition in the painter's craft itself. The interpretation of the contents would indeed have been well-nigh impossible had the translators not already possessed some working knowledge of the methods described in the text—such as the making of parchment size, the preparation of oils and varnishes, the grinding of pigments with their appropriate media and other processes which, though in the past, matters of daily studio routine, no longer form part of an artists' training. Thus, it will be seen, that the experience gained by the actual handling of the substances referred to in the Manuscript, together with the observation of their behaviour under varying conditions has contributed to the understanding of much that might otherwise have remained incomprehensible. Furthermore, such working knowledge has been the means of correcting some of those small slips of the pen which are bound to occur here and there in a document of this kind and which sometimes tend to mislead the reader.

Of recent years many new editions and translations of old painting manuals have appeared in print. Such publications are for the most part welcomed as works of scholarship and are considered as of importance from an antiquarian point of view but they are seldom if ever, except in the case of Cennini's *Trattato*, regarded as having any bearing on the methods in use by artists today. There is, however, a wealth of information contained in these ancient records which, though often obscured by much that is admittedly archaic or irrelevant, has only to be carefully sorted out and sifted to become of real practical value to modern painters—to those, that is, who aim at any degree of permanence in their work.

zwar oft durch Veraltetes und Unwichtiges verunklärt worden ist, und das nur sorgfältig durchgesehen und gesiebt werden müsste, um von wirklich praktischem Wert für moderne Maler zu werden, mindestens für diejenigen, die nach einem gewissen Grad von Dauerhaftigkeit für ihr Werk streben.

Wenn man die grosse Menge von Dokumenten, die der Malkunst gewidmet sind und die uns über Jahrhunderte hinweg überliefert wurden, der Betrachtung unterzieht, stellt es sich als einwandfrei klar heraus, dass diese an sich nicht aus literarischen Gründen geschrieben wurden, sondern dass sie tatsächlich nur Sammlungen von praktischen Anweisungen, oft in Gestalt von Notizen, sind, die der Meister der Malerschule seinen Lehrlingen als praktische Hilfe für ihre Werkstatt-Arbeit übergab. Wenn man ausserdem vergliechende Studien dieser frühen Manuale macht, kommt man zu dem unvermeidlichen Schluss, dass sie wieder und wieder von einander abgeschrieben worden sind, zuerst in den Klöstern, den kulturellen Zentren der frühen Zeit, und später in den vielen weltlichen Malschulen, die in verschiedenen Teilen des europäischen Kontinents hervorwuchsen.

Man könnte erwarten, dass die eigentlichen Methoden und Materialien, die in diesen frühen Schriften erwähnt werden, sehr verschiedenartig sein würden, da sie aus so unterschiedlichen Quellen stammen. Man findet aber im Gegenteil, dass diese Berichte überraschend gleichartig sind, sowohl mit Bezug auf den behandelten Gegenstand als auch auf die Art ihrer Darstellung, — ganz gleich, ob sie in lateinischer, deutscher, französischer oder in irgendeiner andern europäischen Sprache geschrieben sind. Cennini's Abhandlung *Il Libro del Arte*, die schon vorher erwähnt wurde und die von Mrs. Merrifield im Jahre 1844 erstmalig ins Englische übersetzt wurde, bildet immer noch die Grundlage, auf welcher die Technik moderner Tempera-und Freskomalerei sich aufbaut. Die in dieser Abhandlung enthaltenen Lehren umfassen das gesamte Gebiet der Malerei im Mittelalter; man hat keinerlei Gründe anzunehmen, dass, weil sie in Italien geschrieben wurde, hier nur Methoden, die in Südeuropa benutzt wurden, beschrieben worden sind. Man hat gelegentlich versucht, die Theorie aufzustellen, dass wegen klimatischer Unterschiede im Süden Europa's völlig andere Malmethoden im Gebrauch gewesen wären als die im Norden üblichen. Dieser Ansicht scheint jedoch die grosse Ähnlichkeit zu widersprechen, die sich zwischen den meisten Rezepten aus Manuskripten sowohl nördlicher als auch südlicher Herkunft feststellen lässt. Abgesehen davon, dass der Maler des Nordens mehr dazu neigte, in Öl oder

When we consider the great mass of documents devoted to the painter's craft which have come down to us over the centuries, it becomes evident that these were not written as literature *per se*, but were in fact merely collections of practical instructions, often in the form of notes, given by the Master-Painter to his apprentices to help them in their workshop practice. A comparative study of these early handbooks moreover, leads inevitably to the conclusion that they were copied time and again one from another, first in the monasteries, the centres of cultural activities in early times, and later in the many secular schools of painting which sprang up in various parts of the continent of Europe.

As regards the actual methods and materials mentioned in these early writings, one might have expected that these would have differed widely, coming as they did from such various sources; but on the contrary, we find that both in the matter they contain and in the actual manner of their presentation these records are suprisingly alike—whether written in Latin, German, French or any other European language. Reference has been made above to Cennini's treatise *Il Libro dell' Arte*, which, first translated into English by Mrs. Merrifield in 1844, still forms the basis on which the techniques of modern termpera and fresco are founded. The teaching comprised in its pages covers the whole field of the craft of painting in medieval times and there is no reason to suppose that because it was written in Italy it describes a practice followed in Southern Europe alone. The theory is sometimes advanced that, owing to climatic conditions, quite different painting methods were in use in the South of Europe as compared with those current in the North. This view, however, would seem to be contradicted by the close resemblance that is to be noticed between most of the recipes belonging to manuscripts of both Northern and Southern origin. Apart from the fact that the Northern painter inclined more towards painting in oils or size while his Southern counterpart favoured more generally the use of egg tempera, the difference in methods and materials between North and South appear to have been of only minor importance. Indeed the constant corroboration of one record by another leaves little room for doubt that during the Middle Ages the basic rules for the practice of painting were almost identical throughout Europe.

To return to the Strasburg Manuscript itself, this is evidently one of those painters' handbooks written by the Master for his pupils and intended as a guide in their day to day work in the *bottega*. Although the name of the author (or authors) is not known, it can be inferred from the manner in which it is written that it came from the hand of a

Pergamentleim zu malen, während sein südlicher Fachgenosse es im allgemeinen vorzog, die Ei-Tempera zu benutzen, scheint der Unterschied bezüglich Methoden und Materialien zwischen Nord und Süd nur gering gewesen zu sein. Tatsächlich lässt auch die immer wieder neue Bestätigung eines Berichtes durch einen anderen kaum einen Zweifel darüber, dass die fundamentalen Regeln für die Ausübung der Malkunst im Mittelalter fast die gleichen in ganz Europa waren.

Über das Manuskript selbst wäre zu sagen, dass es augenscheinlich eines jener Malhandbücher ist, die vom Meister für seine Schüler geschrieben wurden, als Anleitungen für ihre täglichen Arbeiten in der *bottega*. Trotzdem der Name des Autors (oder der Autoren) unbekannt ist, ergibt es sich aus der Art des Textes, dass es von der Hand eines ausübenden Künstlers stammt. Er beschreibt nicht nur gewisse Arbeitsweisen im kleinsten Detail, sondern er begleitet seine Anweisungen sogar mit gelegentlichen Ermahnungen und beschwört seine Schüler hier und da, gewisse Dinge geheimzuhalten, als 'Werkstattgeheimnisse'.

Über den eigentlichen Inhalt des Manuskriptes wäre zu sagen, dass die in ihm enthaltenen Belehrungen nicht alle aus einer einzigen Quelle stammen. Die Reihe der in dem Dokument enthaltenen Rezepte scheint in verschiedene Teile zu zerfallen. Der erste Teil enthält die Anweisungen von Heinrich von Lubbege (Lübeck) und behandelt das Herstellen und Zerreiben von Farbstoffen sowie das Mischen von Farbtönen, die man für Illuminierung benutzte. Der zweite Teil schildert Methoden, die man von einem Maler namens Andres von Colmar erlernt hatte, und hier findet man weitere Belehrungen und dazu detaillierte Anweisungen für die Kunst des Vergoldens auf Pergament und über die Herstellung von Gummilösungen, Tinten und Wasserfarben. Der nächste Teil ist der längste und vielleicht der wichtigste. Er enthält eine Fülle von praktischen Lehren für Herstellung von Farben und die Art und Weise ihrer Verwendung. Hier werden Rezepte für Herstellung von Beizen, von verschiedenartigen klebenden Grundierungsmitteln und von Firnis gegeben, mit Anweisungen für das Applizieren von Blattgold oder Silber auf verschiedenen Stoffen. Die Zubereitung von Ölfarben wird ebenfalls im Detail beschrieben, und diese Tatsache bestätigt die jetzt allgemein für annehmbar gehaltene Theorie, dass Ölmalerei als solche in Nordeuropa in allgemeinem Gebrauch lange Zeit vor den Brüdern van Eyck war.

In der vorliegenden Übersetzung des Strassburger Manuskripts haben die Autoren den alten deutschen Text Seite an Seite mit der

practising artist. Not only does he describe certain processes in minute detail but he also accompanies his descriptions with occasional words of warning and here and there adjures his pupils to keep certain matters secret, as 'tricks of the trade'.

In turning to the actual contents of the Manuscript it will be seen that the teaching it comprises does not all come from a single source. The series of receipts this document contains would appear to fall into several parts. The first of these gives the instructions of Heinrich von Lubbege (Lubeck) and deals with the making and grinding of pigments and with the mixing of tints used for illumination, the second part gives methods learnt from a painter of the name of Andrew von Colmar, and in this section further instructions for illuminating appear with the addition of detailed information as to the art of gilding on parchment and concerning the making of gum mediums, inks and water colours. The next part is the longest and perhaps the most important. It is full of practical information concerning the preparation of colours and the manner of their application. Receipts are given for the making of mordants, of several kinds of size and varnish with directions for applying gold or silver leaf on various substances. The preparation of oil colours is also given in some detail and this fact affords confirmation of the now generally accepted theory that oil painting as such was in general use in Northern Europe long before the time of the brothers Van Eyck.

With regard to the arrangement of the present translation of the Strasburg Manuscript the old German text is here set side by side with the English rendering, in order to facilitate comparison of the one with the other. Although the translation has, for the most part, been kept as literal as possible, it will be noticed that in certain passages a freer interpretation has been adopted with the object of making the text more readable and in the hope of bringing out the essential meaning of the original. The old German dialect in which the document is written appears to have been prolix in the extreme and for this reason some of the tedious repetition of words, and even, here and there, of whole phrases has been discarded. This does not mean, however, that any detail necessary to the proper working of any recipe has been omitted; each process described being given in its entirety.

As to those few passages which owing to the use of archaisms still remain obscure, an attempt has been made in the translation to suggest the probable meaning. In the case of single words, however, such as obsolete weights and measures, chemical terms, etc. which have been found impossible to translate, these have been inserted

Übertragung ins Englische angeordnet, um Vergleiche beider Versionen miteinander zu erleichtern. Obgleich die Übersetzung grösstenteils so wörtlich wie möglich gehalten wurde, wird man bemerken, dass bei gewissen Wendungen eine freiere Übersetzung nötig war, um den Text lesbarer zu machen, in der Hoffnung, damit die eigentliche Bedeutung des Originaltextes klar herauszubringen. Der alte deutsche Dialekt, in dem das Manuskript abgefasst worden ist, macht einen ausserordentlich weitschweifigen Eindruck, und daher sind langweilige Wiederholungen von Worten und gelegentlich sogar von ganzen Redewendungen weggelassen worden. Dies bedeutet aber keineswegs, dass irgend ein Detail, das zum Ausarbeiten eines Rezeptes nötig wäre, fortgelassen worden ist; jeder beschriebene Vorgang wurde ohne jede Kürzung wiedergegeben.

Es ist in der Übersetzung versucht worden, auf die wahrscheinliche Bedeutung der wenigen Stellen, die wegen altertümlicher Redewendungen unverständlich sind, hinzuweisen. Einzelne Worte hingegen, wie veraltete Gewichte und Maasse, chemische Bezeichnungen etc., die nicht übersetzt werden konnten, sind unverändert in den englischen und deutschen Text aufgenommen worden, ganz gleich, ob sie ursprünglich deutsch oder lateinisch sind. Wo aber tatsächlich Lücken im deutschen Text vorkommen, konnte man nur versuchen zu erraten, welches Wort oder welche Worte fehlen. Diese Versuch, den Sinn klarzustellen, findet der Leser unter den Anmerkungen am Ende des Buches.

Zur Erleichterung des Lesens wurde eine grundlegende Änderung in der Anordnung des Textes gemacht; d.h. der Teil des Manuskripts, der Dinge von solcher Verschiedenartigkeit wie Seifen-Zubereitung, kosmetische Rezepte und allerlei Haushaltswinke enthält, wurde aus seiner ursprünglichen Position zwischen dem Schluss von Andres von Colmar's Lehren und dem Abschnitt über harzartige Bindemittel, der auf Seite 42 beginnt, entfernt. Er befindet sich jetzt am Ende dieser Arbeit als 'Anhang', d.h. direkt vor den Anmerkungen. Der Zweck dieser Änderung ist, alle Anweisungen, die sich mit der Kunst des Malens befassen, strikt zusammenzuhalten, während alles, was von wenig oder keinem Wert für unsere moderne Zeit ist, an das Ende dieser Arbeit verwiesen wurde.

16

into the English text, as they stand, whether in German or in Latin. Again, where actual lacunae occur in the German, it has only been possible to hazard a guess as to what the missing word or words may have been and these suggested clarifications are to be found among the Notes at the end of the book.

For the convenience of readers, one alteration has been made in the sequence of the text; *i.e.* the section of the Manuscript dealing with such miscellaneous subjects as soap-making, cosmetic preparations and other household hints has been taken away from its original position between the end of the teaching of Andrew von Colmar and the section on gum mediums commencing on page 42. This is now to be found at the end of the work, as an Appendix, *i.e.* immediately before the Notes. The object of this alteration is to keep together all the receipts strictly concerned with the art of the painter, while relegating to the end those which can be of little or no value in modern times.

THE STRASBURG MANUSCRIPT
DIE STRASSBURGER MANUSKRIPT

DIS IST VON VARWEN die mich lert meister Heinrich von lübbegge.

Wiltu lazur machen so legs uff einen stein und nimm den tutter von einem eije und rib es recht wol und tu enwenig Wassers dar zu ist das es truknet[1] uff dem stein so tu es in ein nuschal[2] und flösse es recht wol also dik mit Wasser untz es schön wirt und nim den gumi[3] und rib es uff einen stein und temperer es mit Wasser und tu es in das horn[4] und ouch den lazur und enwenig honges so gat es gern von der fedren so hastu schön fin lazur.

Kom wiltu grün machen so nim enwenig gumi arab. und rib das uff einen stein und tp [tempier] das mit essich und nim spangrün und rib es under enander und darunder geweichten saffran der in essich geweicht si.

Wiltu zinober[5] tempereren ze incorpiereren so rib den zinober mit Wasser und tu dis tutters usz dem eije dar zu und so du es wol geribest so nim eyger clor[6] und temperer es damit.

Wiltu lazur flössen so nim kalk und las den über nacht stan und schüt den das Wasser hübschlichen oben abe und tu daz under den lazur und darnach nim lougen[7] die tribet den kalk us — und tu dar nach Wasser dar an und la daz stan uber nacht daz das Wasser dar uss gang.

Wiltu zinober tempereren ze florirende so nim den zinober und rib in trothen recht wol und nim dann enwenig Wassers und enwenig saffrans[8] und rib es aber dann als vor und nim 2 troph tutters und rib das do mit und tu es dann in das horn und t̄p̄er [tempier] es dann mit eyger clor und die materie la dik.

Nim zinober und enwenig criden und enwenig saffrans und 6 troph tutters und rib daz recht wol mit eyger clor und t̄p̄er es mit eiger clor.

So du lazur kouffen wilt so nim der recht brun[9] si dar nach so du in tpereren wilt so rib in recht wol mit eigern tuttern und purgiers mit lougen und lasse es wol gesitzen und schütte daz oben ab in ein ander horn und schüt es als wol dik uff und ab untz das es luter werd und las es truknen wol und tu es den in ein seklin und gehaltz wie lang du wilt und wenn du opiereren wilt damitte so tu es in ein horn und tper es mit starkem gumi und 2 troph tutters von einem eige und lass es gestan einen tag und wellost du denne so tu enwenig rouselin dar under hest du gern brun blau.

Dis ist die floritur des lazures. Nim daz ab dem lazur ist kommen und tu es in ein hörnelin und tu dar zu enwenig rouselin und 1 troph tuttern und la die materie dik und opier damit so du wilt und tper. es mit gumi.

HEREIN IS SET DOWN all the teaching about colours that was given me by the Master-Painter, Henry of Lubeck.

If you wish to prepare blue pigment, lay it on a grinding slab and taking the yolk of an egg grind it thoroughly with the blue adding a little water to it. When it is dry[1] on the slab, put it into a pot[2] and wash it well with water till it is nice and clean. Then take gum arabic[3] and grind it on your slab and dilute it with water. Put this in an ink-pot[4] and add your blue and also a little honey. This will give you a lovely bright blue which will flow well from the pen.

Now if you want to make green, take a little gum arabic and grind it on a slab mixing it with vinegar. Then take verdigris and grind them all together with some saffron which has been softened by soaking in vinegar.

If you wish to temper vermilion[5] for laying a flat wash, grind the vermilion in water and then add egg-yolk to it and when you have ground it well take white of egg[6] (glaire) and temper your vermilion with it.

If you wish to purify blue by washing, take lime and let it stand overnight with water over it and then carefully pour off the surplus water on to the blue. Then take lye[7] to get rid of the lime. Afterwards pour clean water on the blue and let it stand overnight to enable the pigment to sink to the bottom.

If you want to temper vermilion for making fine flourishes, take the pigment and grind it well in a dry state. Then take a little water and a little saffron[8] and grind as before, adding two drops of egg-yolk. Grind all together and put it in a pot. Temper it, when you want to use it, with glaire and use it rather thick.

Take vermilion, a little chalk and a little saffron and six drops of egg-yolk and grind it very thoroughly with glaire. Also dilute for use with glaire.

When you buy blue, choose one that is of a deep[9] tint. When you want to temper it, grind it well with yolk of egg, then wash it with lye and leave it to stand. Then pour off the surplus liquid into another pot and continue this process of washing the colour until it becomes clean. Let it dry well and then put it in a little bag and keep it as long as you like. When you want to use it, put some in an ink-pot and temper it with strong gum and two drops of egg-yolk and let it settle for a day. If you require a warmer blue, add a little rose colour.

The following is the mixture for making flourishes with blue. Take the water you drew off the top of the blue and put it in a small pot. Add a little pink and one drop of egg-yolk to it, and, keeping it rather thick, use it for whatever you require, tempering it with gum.

Dis ist ein gele varwe von opiment[10]. Nim zu dem ersten opiment und rib es recht wol truken und nim dar zu eiger tutter und enwenig saffrans und rib es recht wol und tu es dann in ein hörnelin und opier damit und tper es mit eyger clor.

Wiltu machen rosolin von grund uff so nim I lot[11] geschabz brisil[12] holtz und I loth alan und rib den als wol als mel und als vil criden als des alantz und rib ouch die lang und leg jegliches ze einem huffelin und nim ein glas[13] und bespreng das mit enwenig alant und dar nach mit also vil criden und denne dar uff also vil prisil holtzes und schütte dar uff wol geschlagen eiger clor das — es denn über gange und lasse es dann stan 8 Tag und truke es durch ein tuch rech wol in den criden stein und lass es derren in einer Wermi und nim die materie und tu si gehalten in ein sekelin und so du opiereren wilt so tpier es mit Wasser.

Wiltu lazur t̄p̄īēr̄e daz es klein und vin us der fedren gat so nim zu dem ersten des lazures als vil du wilt und rib das uff einen stein mit starkem gumi wasser und mit eigers tutter untz das es nüt uff dem stein crostele und tu es zemol in ein zinie schüssel und güsse starke heisse louge dar über und zerrib das lazur unter die lougen gar wol und las es ein willin stan untz das es zu boden sitzet und güs daz oberste oben abe in ein ander schüssel und güss es den in die ersten schüssel aber der heissen lougen und tu im ze glicherwise als und tu das 3 stunt oder 4 stunt untz das die lougen luter wirt und von dem Wasser luter gange und darnach so güss luter wasser uff die lazur und las es gesitzen und sige das Wasser genot von dem lazur so its daz lazur klein und wol bereit.

Wiltu schön vin grün tempiereren so nim vin spangrün als vil du wilt und rib daz gar wol mit essich da rinne gumi arab. zergangen si und a so gros wassers von winstein[14] als ein erwis do von wirt daz grün satt und glantz und drie troph. eiger tutter und zwen blumen saffrans dis rib alles under enander daz es us gerne ganage.

Wiltu schön ruberik machen. Nim zinober als vil du wilt und rib den Zinober uff einen reinen stein mit Wasser gar wol und wenn du es geribest daz es gar roth bi truken[15] si uff dem stein so nim 3 troph. des tutters uff dem stein un nim den des andern Wassers daz uff dem eiger clor ist gemacht und nim des uff den stein als das die varwe wol nass werde und rib es dar nach uff dem stein als under enander und[16] daz von dem stein in ein rein horn und rur es mit einem reinen höltzelin under enander und versuche es mit einer fedren gat es nit us der fedren so ist die tint ze dik so sol man me klores usser dem glas tun in das horn und soll es aber ruren und versuchen bis daz es recht wirt als du die fedren in das horn tust als

The following is a yellow made from orpiment[10]. First of all take orpiment and grind it thoroughly in a dry state and add to it egg-yolk and a little saffron. Grind them well together and put the colour in a little pot. For use, dilute with glaire.

If you want to make pink—the whole process from start to finish—take ½ oz.[11] of brazil[12] wood shavings and ½ oz. alum ground as fine as flour; then add the same amount of chalk and grind this also thoroughly. Now place each of these in a little heap, and taking a glass[13], sprinkle in a little of the alum and after this the same quantity of the chalk and then the same quantity of the Brazil wood and pour over them well beaten white of egg until they are covered. Leave the mixture to stand for eight days and then strain it well through a cloth into an earthenware vessel, and let it dry in a warm place. Then take it up and keep it in a bag and when you want to use it, dilute it with pure water.

If you wish to temper blue so that it flows freely from the pen, first take the quantity of blue you require and grind it on the slab with strong gum water and with egg-yolk in order that it may not set on the slab, and put it immediately into a tin vessel and pour strong, hot lye on it and stir the blue well together with the lye. Leave it standing for a while, till the pigment settles at the bottom of the vessel, then pour the supernatent liquid off into another bowl. Next, pour into the first vessel (*i.e.* the one with the blue pigment in it) more hot lye and repeat the above process of letting the pigment settle and of pouring off the liquid three or four times until it (*i.e.* the lye) when poured off becomes quite clear. Lastly pour clean water on the blue pigment and let it settle at the bottom of the vessel, then strain the water off well. This will give you a blue which is finely ground and well prepared.

When you want to prepare a lovely bright green, take well ground verdigris, whatever quantity you need, and grind it thoroughly in vinegar in which gum arabic has been dissolved and add as much powdered tartar[14] as a pea. This will make the green deep and lustrous. Then take three drops of egg-yolk and two saffron flowers and grind these all together and you will find that it flows well from the pen.

When you want to make a red for ruberics, take vermilion, as much as you need, and grind it thoroughly on a clean grinding stone with water and when you have ground it so that it looks a good red[15] when it dries on the slab, add three drops of egg-yolk, with a little of the medium which is made from white of egg. Pour enough of this on the slab to make the colour very liquid, grinding all well

dik sol tu es ruren.

Wiltu machen ein gut fundament[17] dar uff man silber und golt leit daz es schön und glantz werde. Nim zu dem ersten cretam pellicarie das ist die die Kürsener hant die sie criden sol man also bereiten man sol nemen hecht schuppen und hecht gebein von dem houpt und das sol man under enander sieden in einer überlazurt kachlen als lang bis das der drittel in gesiede dar nach sol man brüge sigen durch ein linine tuch und rib die vorgen criden mit der visch brüge und tu es denne in ein nuschal und lasse es denne hert werden und wenne du wilt ein fundament machen ze gold so nim der vorgen criden die bereit si als gros als ein haselnus und rib die gar wol uff einen stein mit dem Wasser das von dem eiger clor si gemacht und rib darunder ouch als gros zinobers als ein erwis und salis armonic. ouch als ein erwis und 3 blumen saffrans das rib gar wol alles under enander uff einen stein und tu es von dem stein in ein nuschal dis soltu tempiereren in der diki als ein ruberik dis hört zu vim golde ze glicherwise mag man silber daruff legen also daz der saffran nut dar under komme und dis sol man nass[18] uff legen.

Wiltu machen ein gut fundament gold und silber uff ze legen truken.[19] So nim ze glicherwise als viel criden als vor und rib daz ze glicherwise als das erst und tu dar under zinober als gros als ein erwis salis armoniak ouch als vil und 2 troph honges und rib das alles gar wol under enander mit dem Wasser das uss dem eiger clor ist gemacht und tpier, es under enander in der diki als ein ruberik und tu es dar nach in ein rein nuschal und merk wo du daz wilt uff schriben so sol man es vorhin under enander wol ruren und sol man daz berment vorhin wol purnieren da man gold varwe hin welle schriben und wenn man die gold varwe uff strichen will so sol man si blos uff strichen und gar gelich. Dis ist ein assis silber und gold truken uff ze legende.

Nim heideschen Ziegel[20] den die Gold smit hant und enwenig kolen und rib das wol und 1 troph honges oder zwen darzu und tpier daz mit lin von husen blatern gesotten und leg gold daruff troken.

together. Then take[16] it up from the stone and put it in a clean ink-pot. Mix it well round with a clean wooden stick and try it in your pen. If it does not flow easily from the pen, the ink is too thick and you must add more of the liquid glaire out of the glass into your pot and stir it again and test it, till it is of the right consistency when you dip the pen into the ink-pot. Continue stirring till it is right.

If you want to make a good foundation[17] on which to lay silver and gold, so that they are beautifully smooth—first of all take *cretam pellicarie* which the furriers stock. This chalk is prepared in the following way. Take the scales and bones, preferably those of the head, of a pike, and boil them together in a double-glazed vessel until the liquid is reduced by a third, then strain the brew through a linen cloth and grind the above-mentioned chalk with the fish-brew. Put it in a pot and let it harden and when you want to make the foundation for gold-leaf, take a piece the size of a hazel-nut of this preparation and grind it well on the slab with some glaire. Grind into this equal quantities, both the size of a pea, of vermilion and sal-ammoniac and three saffron flowers. Grind this all well together on a slab and put it in a pot. It should be diluted to the same consistency as ink for ruberics. This foundation is right for laying under gold-leaf; for silver-leaf the process is the same except that the saffron is omitted. The leaf should be laid by the wet[18] method.

If you want to make a good foundation on which gold and silver can be laid by the dry[19] method—take the same amount of chalk as before and grind it in the same manner as for the last recipe. Add to it vermilion and sal-ammoniac in equal quantities, the size of a pea, and two drops of honey. Grind these well together with liquid glaire and mix them to the same consistency as for ruberics. Put this mordant in a clean pot and be careful always to stir the mixture well before applying it, and also to burnish the parchment well before laying it. When you want to use it, just paint it on very evenly. It should be dry when the gold or silver leaf is applied.

Take finest Lemnian[20] earth which the goldsmiths keep and a little charcoal and grind it well with one or two drops of honey. Temper this with soaked fish glue and lay the gold leaf by the dry method.

Dis lehrt mich Meister Andres von Colmar.

So du wilt einen grund machen ze übergülden so nim criden und stosse die und leg si in ein schüsselin und la si dar inne zwene tag und schüt den das Wasser oben ab und nim die criden und rib si uff einen reinen stein und mache lim dar us und leg si uff ein schindelen und la sie truknen. So du denne übergülden wilt so nim zwen teil criden und den dritteil sal armoniak so er iemer wissest mag sin und schabe von einer zechen huse blatern als gros als ein linsin und ein vil wenig honges und tu das dar under und tper. das alles mit Wasser.

Wiltu uff vin gold florieren das es recht zierlich stat als das ein gold uff das ander wer geflorieret. Nim in der apeteke gumi ara. als gros als zwo erwis und zerschnid das zu kleinen stükelin und güs wissen essich dar über in ein nuschal und la das stan über nacht ze weichen und sege den essich oben abe und nim das gewerkt gumi arab. und tu es uff einen reinen stein und rib es enklein und tpers in der diki als ein ruberik mit itelm wasser und tu es dar nach in die nuschal und florier damit in gold daz stat gar zierlich und wol.

Nim eines Salmen gallen oder eines lachsengalle und strich die galle uff ein nuschale und tu ein troph essichs dar under und florier da mit uff gold das dritte so nim verger von Metz und rib das uff einen reinen stein mit enwenig Wassers de gumi arab. Daz hienach verschriben stat daz soltu verhelen.

Wiltu guldin geschrifft machen. Nim in der appotek aurum musitum [21] und rib das mit Wasser uff einen reinen stein gar wol und nim des Wassers de gumi arab. ein teil und den andern teil gemeines Wassers und zertrib die zwei Wasser mit dem finger under enander in einer reinen nuschal und das triben aurum muscatum in die nuschal und zertrib es under enander in der diki als ein ruberick. Und schrib domit was du wilt und las das truken werden und purnier das senfteklichen mit einem glatten Zan von einem wolf so wirt die geschrifft schön und glantz gold werden.

Wellent ir silbrin geschrift haben margasitan argenteam und ribent das mit wasser gar wol und klein und so es wol geriben werde so tund es von dem steine in ein grosse nuschal und güs die nuschal vol Wassers und rur es mit einem finger wol under enander und las es den enklein ze boden sitzen und güs den des obersten wassers dar ab von der nuschale und tu aber me Wassers dar in und menge es under enander und las es aber enwenig gesitzen und güs des obersten Wassers aber darab bis daz es luter werde und nim den des Wassers des gumi arab. ein teil und des andern teil gemeins Wassers und müsche die zwei wasser ze sammen und tpiers damit ze glicherwise in der diki als ein ruberik und schrib domit was du wilt und las das

The following teaching was given me by the Master-Painter Andrew of Colmar.

If you want to make a foundation for gilding, take chalk and crush it and put it in a small bowl covered with water and leave it for two days. Then pour off the water and grind the chalk to a paste on a clean slab and put it on a little wooden board and let it dry. When you want to gild take two parts of this chalk and one part sal-ammoniac in order to make it whiter. Then taking a leaf of dried fish glue, shave off a tiny piece the size of a lentil and add a very little honey. Mix these all together and temper with water.

If you want to make flourishes on a plain gold ground to make it more decorative and give the effect of a gold pattern over a gold ground, procure gum arabic from the apothecary, the size of two peas, and crush it up into very small fragments. Put this gum into a pot, pour white vinegar over it and leave it to stand softening overnight. Then strain off the surplus vinegar and put the prepared gum arabic on the grinding slab and grind it a little and dilute it with this medium to the same consistency as for ruberics and put it in a pot and flourish with it on the gold. This gives a very rich effect.

Take the gall of a salmon and put it in a pot and add a drop of vinegar and flourish with it on gold. A third way—take ochre from Metz and grind it on a clean slab with a little liquified gum arabic.

The process I am now going to describe must be kept secret. If you want to make a golden writing, procure *aurum musitum*[21] from the apothecary and grind it thoroughly on a clean slab with water. Take one part of liquid gum arabic and one part water and mix them together in a clean pot, with the finger, then add this to the ground up *aurum musitum* and mix them together till they are of the same consistency as for ruberics and write anything you wish with this and let it dry. Then burnish it gently with a well polished wolf's tooth and the writing will look like burnished gold.

If you want to have silver writing, take *margasitan argenteam* and grind it well with water till it is very finely ground, then take it from the slab and put it in a large pot and fill it up with water and mixing it well together with the finger, leave it a little while to settle. Then pour off the surplus water and fill up with more, stirring again. Then let it settle for a short time and again pour off the surplus liquid and continue doing so until the water becomes clear. Then take equal quantities of liquified gum arabic and of pure water and mix them together and dilute to the same consistency as for ruberics, and write whatever you wish with it. Let it dry, and burnish it with a polished wolf's tooth and your writing will be as bright and shining

truken werden und punier es mit einem glatten Wolf Zan so wirt die geschrift schön und glantz silber var.

Dis ist das dritte wie man gold und silber schribet us der fedren. Nim in der Appentegen punicem romanam und rib das uff einen reinen stein gar klein und wol mit Wasser und nim dis Wassers in dem ersten glas des gumi arab. ein teil und also vil brunnen Wassers und tpier. es under enander in der diki als ein ruberik und schrib was du wilt und wenne daz gar wol truken ist so nim vin gold und rib daz uff die geschrift senfteclich bis daz die geschrift über al geverwt si worden dar nach so nim des Wolfes Zan und überwar die geschrift ouch senfteclich überal bis daz es schön und glantz werde. Wiltu das Silbervar machen so übervar die geschrift mit silber und darnach ouch mit dem zan so wirt si schön und glantz.

Wiltu aber gold und silber schriben us der fedren so nim 20 bletter[22] von golde oder vier u. zwanzig zu dem meisten und leg die bletter alle nebent enander uff den stein und nim saltz und übersaltz die bletter überal darnach so nim starken wissen essich und über spreng die bletter und las es ein wil also ligen und rib es darnach gar wol und tpiers. mit dem gumi. ara.°° und ein teil gemeines Wassers und rib es denne mit einen zan das golde.

Wie man ein Wasser[23] machet damit man alle varwen sol tempieren. Nim in der Apeteke ein specie heisset gumi arab. ein lot oder als vil du wilt und leg das in ein linin tuch und winde das ze sammen und blewe das bis das es ze bulver werde in dem tuch darnach so tu das bulver us dem tuch in ein überlazurt kachlen die rein si und güs dar über schön Wasser das eins fingers dik darüber gang und las daz also stan über nacht bis das es weich wirt und zertrib es mit einem finger gar wol under einander und leg darzu ein settit wisser mirren die luter si und las das ouch in dem Wasser stan und zergan und zich es denn dar ein rein linin tüchlin und dis Wasser tu in ein glas bis man sin bedarff. dis Wasser sol als dik sin als öli.

Nim das clor von 2 eigern in ein rein Schüsselen und Kloph das eiger clor mit al einem löffel bis es dünne werde und nim einen schönen badstein[24] und ring das clor dar durch zo v. malen bis das es nümma schümi darnach nim gumi ara. ein settit und leg das in dem eiger clor und las es zergan und nim darnoch ein gefügen Löfel vol essichs und zertrib das under das clor und leg darnoch in das clor als gros salis armonic. als ein erwis di Wasser du besunder in ein glas auch wol behalten bis man sin ouch bedarff.

Wellent ir schön fin tuchlin[25] varwe[26] machen so nim in den ersten 8 Tagen nach pfingsten 7[27] voll korn blumen die an dem morgent gewunnen sint vor mittem tag und brich die blumen oben ab in ein

28

as real silver.

This is a third way to write with gold and silver from a quill pen. Procure from the apothecary *punicem Romanam* [light red Roman earth] and grind it thoroughly on a clean slab with water. Take the liquid from the first glass which contains equal quantities of gum arabic and well water and mix it, with the paste from the slab, to the consistency of ink for ruberics. Write whatever you wish with it and when it is quite dry, take fine gold-leaf and lay it over the writing, pressing down very gently until all the writing is covered with gold.

Finally later take a wolf's tooth and rub over all the writing very gently, till it becomes bright and shining. If you want the writing to be silver, lay silver-leaf instead of gold, burnishing in the same way with the tooth afterwards.

If you want to write with gold and silver in your quill, take 20 leaves[22] or 24 at most, and lay them one beside the other on the slab and take salt and sprinkle it all over them. Then take strong white vinegar and spray the leaves with it and leave them for a little while. Next grind them well together and temper with the usual mixture of half gum arabic and half pure water. Finally when the writing is done, polish the gold with the tooth.

How to make a medium[23] for tempering all your colours. Procure from the apothecary a balsam called gum arabic, $\frac{1}{2}$ oz. or as much as you want and put it in a linen cloth and twist and pound it till it is reduced to powder in the cloth. Then put the powder from the cloth into a glazed receptacle, which must be very clean and pour over it clear water to the height of a finger's breadth and let it stand overnight to soften. Mix it well with the water with a finger and add a *settit* of white myrrh and let this also soak in the same water till it melts, then strain it through a linen cloth. This medium should be as thick as oil.

Put the whites of two eggs in a clean dish and beat with a spoon till they are liquid and take a clean linen[24] towel and wring the white of egg through it time after time, until it ceases to foam. Then take one *settit* of gum arabic and put it in the egg white and let it melt, next take a good spoonful of vinegar and mix it with the glaire and add to this as much sal ammoniac as a pea. Be sure to keep this medium always in a glass jar or bottle till it is required.

If you want to make a bright rag[25] colour[26], proceed as follows. During the first week after Whitsun pick a quantity[27] of fully opened cornflowers—these should be gathered during the morning, that is, before midday. Break off the flowers at the top of the stem, put them in a clean vessel and pound them in a clean mortar very thoroughly,

rein geschir und stosse die blumen oben ab in ein reinen Mursel gar
wol bis das si werdent als ein müs dar nach leg sie in ein rein zwilch
tuch und ring das safft dur das tuch gar wol in ein überlazurt kachlen
und nim ein settit salis armoniaci und leg es in die varwe so zergat
es zehant darnach da nim ein schön wol geweschen tuch von einem
alten sleiger oder von einem alten tischlachen und stos der tüchlin in
die varwe als das das tuch die varwe alle an sich zieche als das die
tücher weder ze nas noch ze dür werdent und süd die varwe untz das
si überal habend emphangen und darnach sol man die tücher
nebent enander henken in einen reinen garten an den wint und las si
wol truken werden do noch an den andren morgent so soltu aber der
blumen frisch gewinnen als vil als vor und solt si aber oben ab brechen
und aber stossen ze müs als vor und durch das zwilch tuch ringen in
die und nim denn gumi arab. das gar luter si das vor gewerchen si mit
und das gumi sol man zertriben mit einem finger under enander und
müsch das zertriben gumi under die blumen und rur es mit dem holtz
under enander und nim alunen glaciei ein settit klein zertriben ze
bulver und leg das bulver in das vorgñ safft und rur es wol under
enander bis dass das aluñen zergangen si da noch so nim die vorgñ
geverwten tücher und truk si zu dem andren mol in die varwe und las
si in der varwe bis si die varwe genot an sich ziechent und wol
geverwt sin dar noch so henk die tücher aber uff an den wint und lass
si gar wol truken werden dar nach so wind die tücher in ein schön
papier und leg das gehalten in ein rein new schindelladen und setz es
enbor in den lufft das es nut flüchte habe.

Wiltu violvarw tüchlin machen so nim aber in der selben zit[28] rot
korn blumen als vil du wilt und brich die bletter von den blumen und
stosse sie gar wol und ring das saff dur ein rein linin tuch in ein
überlazurt kacheln und nim aluñe glaciei ein settit ist der blumen vil
ist ir aber lützel so nim dester minder und doch merke hie werde der
blumen ein quertelin so gehort denn ein settit dar in alans wer aber
der blumen nut also vil so lege nut not dar an und ob das settit alans
genot dar in keme dar noch so tu die tücher in die varwe und verwe
si über al noch henke die tücher uff an den wint und las si wol
truken werden und nim der blumen als vil als vor und stosse die
blumen und truk das safft aber dar us durch das tuch und stosse die
tücher aber an daz safft daz si aber wol geverwt werden über al und
zertrib aber in dem safft gumi arab. und henke denn die tücher an
den wint und la si wol truken werdent und winde die tücher in
pappier. Dis heisset violvarw tüchlin.

Wiltu machen brun blau tüchlin varw. Nim heidelber so si ze dem
ersten uff gans ein schüssel vol und tu die ber in ein new hefelin und

till they are reduced to a mash. After this, put them in a clean straining-cloth and wring out the juice into a glazed pan. Then take a *settit* of sal-ammoniac and put it in the coloured juice and it will dissolve at once. After this take a well-washed piece of material, such as a piece of fine old veiling or of an old tablecloth and put this, cut in small pieces, into the colour so that the 'rags' soak up all the coloured liquid and become neither too wet nor too dry but just soak up the colour and are evenly tinted. After this one should hang up the rags on a line in the garden letting them dry well in the open air. The next day, pick the same amount of fresh flowers as before and repeat the process of breaking off the heads of the flowers, of pounding them as before and of wringing the juice through a straining-cloth into the pan. Then take very clear gum arabic, that has been previously softened. This gum must first be well stirred round with the finger and then be mixed with the juice of the flowers and stirred with a wooden stick. Then take one *settit* of alum crystals ground to a fine powder and put this into the above mentioned juice and stir it well until the alum has melted. Then take the already coloured rags (which have been drying overnight) and dip them once again in the juice and leave them steeping in the colour till they have soaked up enough to dye them thoroughly. After this, hang up the rags again in the open air and let them dry thoroughly. Lastly, wrap them up in clean paper and keep them in a clean wooden box somewhere high up and well ventilated, in order that they may not get damp.

If you want to make a violet rag colour you must gather pink cornflowers, at the same time[28] of year—as many as you like—and bruise the petals and grind them well and wring the juice through a clean linen cloth into a glazed pan and take one *settit* of alum crystals; if you have a lot of flowers, that is; but if only a small quantity, take a smaller amount, but you should note that if the flowers amount to a quarter lb. the correct amount of alum would be one *settit*, but if the amount of petals were less, put in less alum. Afterwards put the rags in the colour and dye them very thoroughly, then hang them up in the open air and let them dry well. Now take as many flowers as before and pound the petals and again strain the juice through a cloth. Once again press the rags well down into the juice to tint them evenly, having remembered to add gum arabic to the juice. Now hang out the rags in the air and let them dry well and finally wrap them in paper. This is called violet rag colour.

If you want to make a deep blue rag colour take a bowlful of bilberries, making sure that they are the first crop[?] and put the berries in a glazed jar covered with a lid and sink this in the earth

tu das hefelin wol bedekt in die erden bis under den hals und la si
also stan acht tag bis das si wol in einem reinen mürsel[29] und tu si in
einen reinen nëwen hafen und güs das hefelin vol wassers also das des
Wassers ein quertelin si zu einer schüssel vol ber und rur die ber und
das wasser wol under enander und nim salis armon: I settit und also
vil alus glaciei und setz das hefelin zu dem für und las es senfte-
clichen erwallen das es nut überlöffe wenne es blos erwallet so heb es
von dem für und las es uberschlachen dar noch nim sal aro und
alun glaciei iegliches ein settit und log das in die varwe in den hafen
und lans da in zergan und la die varwe in dem hafen wol kalt
werden dar nach so güs die varwe in dem hafen in ein rein zwilch
tuch und ring die varwe durch das tuch in ein überlazurt kacheln so
blibent die hülschen und die kernen in dem tuch gat in [30] die kacheln
dar nach so nim schön wiss tuch und einen alten sleiger oder von
einem alten tislachen und stos die tücher in varwe das si wol geverwt
werdent und henke die tücher do noch uff an den wint und las si wol
truken werden und tu si du weist wol war.

Wiltu roselin varw machen schön und fin die uff silber und uff
gold durluchtig ist. Nim persilien holtz ein lot oder zwei das wol
klein geschaben si und nim eichen eschen oder buchin und der
zweiger ein und mach ein lougen die da luter und rein si und nim ein
überlazurt kachlen vol lougen und setz es uff ein glut und las die
lougen heis werden also das man ein finger kam darin haben magt und
leg das vorgn̄ holtz in die heissen lougen und truk das holtz under mit
einem höltzlin und ze hant so wirt die loug rot als einer schönen ros
und las das also ein wil stan so ziechet louge die[31] alle ze mal an sich
us dem holtz dar noch so nim alun glaciei ein settit wol klein bulver
zerriben und sege das bulver über das holtz in die varwe und rur es
mit einem holtz wol under enander und seche es den als dur ein lini
tuch in ein rein überlazurt kachlen und las das also stan über nacht
bis das die röti ze boden sitzet und das Wasser das obenan swebet das
güs hüplich oben ab bis uff das dik das kechelin da die diki varwe
rine ist das setz uff den offen und las es also stan bis daz die varwe
dürre si so tu si us dem kechelin in ein blatern behalten bis man in
bedarff were aber der varwe vil 3 lot oder 4 oder ein vierling wenne
denn die varwe bereit wirt und gesigen ist durch das tuch so sol man
si güssen in ein sekelin das sekelin sol dik sin geweben daz man kum
dadur gesicht und sol sin undenan spiccig und obenan wic mit
einem reiff obenan und solt den sak vorhin netzen und wider ringen
und den die vorgn̄ varwe alle in den sak giessen und ein kechelin dar
under setzen und das zu dem ersten us dem sak trüphet das ist
enwenig rot wand es us dem sak luter trophet so güs die varwe in dem

32

as far as the neck and let it stay there about a week till it is . . . in a clean mortar[29] and put them in a glazed jar and fill this with water up to the top, allowing one quart[?] to each bowlful of berries. Stir the berries and water well together and take one *settit* sal-ammoniac and the same quantity of alum crystals and put the pan on the fire and let it cook gently, so that it does not boil over. When it is thoroughly cooked, take it from the fire and leave it to subside. Now take your sal-ammoniac and your alum crystals, a *settit* of each, and put it in the colour which is in the pan and let it dissolve in it and let this colour get quite cold. Afterwards strain the colour into a glazed vessel through a clean cloth leaving hulls and seeds behind. Only the colour[30] goes into the earthenware vessel. After this, take some clean white material such as a piece of old veiling or tablecloth and steep pieces of this material in the colour, so that they are well tinted and then hang them up in the open air to dry thoroughly, as before and you know, by now, where is the best place to keep them.

If you want to make a beautiful bright rose colour, to use as transparent glazing over silver and gold, make this from Brazil wood ($\frac{1}{2}$ oz. or 1 oz.) which has been pared into fine shavings. First of all, take the ashes of oak or beech twigs and make a lye, which must be very bright and clear. Take a glazed earthenware vessel full of this, put it on a glowing fire and let it get so hot that you can hardly bear your finger in it and lay the above-mentioned Brazil wood in the hot lye and push the shavings well down under the liquid with the wooden stirring-rod and immediately the lye will turn a beautiful rosy red—then leave it to stand and in this way the red colouring matter[31] will all be drawn from the wood by the lye. After this, take one *settit* of alum crystals crushed to fine powder and sprinkle this over the wood shavings in the liquid, stir well together with a wooden stick and then strain it through a linen cloth into a clean glazed earthenware vessel. Let it stand overnight until the red sediment settles at the bottom and carefully pour off the surplus liquid till you come to the deposit; the pot with the thick deposit in it you then put in the oven and leave until the colour dries, then take it out of the vessel and put it into a bladder and keep it till required. *N.B.* If the colour, when strained were to be as much as $1\frac{1}{2}$ to 2 ozs. or perhaps a quarter of a pound, you must pour it into a little bag, densely woven so that one can hardly see through it. It (the bag) should be pointed below and be kept wide at the top by means of a stiff rim (like a Church offertory bag). You should moisten the bag first and wring it out and then pour all the colour into the bag and place a bowl underneath it. The liquid that first filters through the

33

52417

kechelin under in den sak und henk den sak uff an einen nagel und setze die kechelen under den sak und la den sak über nacht hangen bis das das Wasser alles us getrüffet und wenne der sak nüt me trüphet so nim ein glat bret oder einen ziegel und wende den sak umb und schab die varwe alle gar wol ab dem sak uff daz bret oder uff den ziegelstein[32] und setz die varwe an den luft drie tag oder 4 untz das si dürre werde dar noch tu si gehalten in ein blatern bis man ir bedarf dis heisset fin röselin varwe.

Wellent ir machen schön fin paris rot. Nim zu dem ersten und mach ein loug us weiss essichen und nim einer specie die heisset lagga[33] damit man das lousch verwert dis sol man zerstossen ze kleinem bulver und sol die lougen heis machen und sol das bulver von dem lagga in die heissen lougen reren und sol das under enander ruren und las es also stan ze beissende über nacht an dem morgent sol man die varwe zu dem für setzen und sol si ruren on underlas und sol sieden halb als lang als man vische sudet und sol den 1 settit aluns glaciei in die varwe tun und sol es wol ruren bis das es zergat dar nach hab die varwe von dem füre und lasse si überslachen und siche die varwe durch ein rein tuch das — zwifelag sig und ring die varwe us in die überlazurt kachlen und nim den alun der gar klein ze bulver si getriben und rer das bulver langsam in die varwe und rur es als mit einem löffel bis das der alun in der varwe wol zergagen si hie merke ein wortzeichen wenn die varwe dikelecht wirt als ein win warm und doch schön rot do mit ist so sol man nüt me aluns dar in reren wenne die varwe dünne ist als wasser so sol man des aluns mer dar in tun und under enander ruren bis das die varwe schön dik werde darnach so güs die varwe al ze mal in einen sak der geformet si als der sak zu der röselin varwe und las den sak also hangen ze trieffen über nacht bis nüt me us dem sak trüfft und was nun us dem sak trüffet das ist als liecht rot win das sol man enwenig giessen aber das in dem sak belibet das ist schön vin rot varwe den sak sol man umb wenden und die varwe uff einen stein tun und mit dem messer die varwe ab dem sak schaben und tun denne die varwe an den wind und las si wol dür werden und tu si denn wol rein behalten bis man ir bedarff.

Wiltu bermit schön vin durlüchtig machen weler varwe du wilt als ein glas so nim des lutersten megdenbermenten[34] des man do vindet und wesche das bermit in kalter lougen gar wol bis das die loug luter und clor von dem bermit gang dar no so wesche es in luterm wasser so ist das bermit luter und clor worden dar nach so ring daz Wasser us dem bermit wiltu nu daz bermit schön fin grun machen das man da dur sicht was man wil als dur ein schön glas so

bag will be slightly red but as soon as the liquid drips through clear you must pour the liquid that is in the bowl back into the bag and hang this up on a nail, putting the bowl underneath it again. Leave the bag hanging up overnight until the rest of the water has all drained out. When the liquid has ceased dripping from the bag, take a smooth board or a tile[32] and turning the bag inside out, scrape off all the colour thoroughly on to the board; put it out in the open air for three or four days until it becomes quite hard. After this keep it carefully in a bladder till required. This pigment is called rose colour.

When you wish to make bright Paris red, start by making a lye from wood ash and then buy the balsam called 'lac'[33] [lake] used for dyeing wool, which must be crushed into fine powder. Sprinkle it into the hot lye, stirring it well together and leave it soaking overnight in order to draw out the colour. In the morning this colour must be put on the fire to boil and stirred constantly and should cook for half as long as one would boil fish; next one *settit* of alum crystals must be added and well stirred until dissolved. Then take the colour from the fire and leave it to subside and strain it through a clean piece of double muslin. Wring out the liquid into a glazed earthenware vessel and take the alum that has been ground to a fine powder and sprinkle it gradually into the colour stirring all together with a spoon till the alum has quite dissolved in the colour. The following 'tip' may be useful to you—if the colour has become as thick as a good mulled wine and is at the same time of a full red tint, there is no need to sprinkle any more alum in, if however the colour is thin like water you should add more alum and stir it well round until the colour is nice and thick. After this, you must pour all the colour into a bag the same shape as that used for the rose colour and leave it hanging up to drip overnight until nothing more drips out. What first drips out of the bag will be like vin rosé and some of this should be poured off but what remains in the bag will be the colour of good red wine. The colour must now be transferred to a stone slab by turning the bag inside out, any remaining colour being scraped from the bag with a knife. Next put the colour in the open air and let it get really hard and put it somewhere to be kept clean until required.

If you want to make parchment as transparent as glass and of any colour you wish, take the most translucent vellum[34] you can find and wash it well in cold lye until after repeated washings the lye comes away clear and clean, then rinse in pure water till the parchment is quite clean and finally press the water out thoroughly. Then if you want to tint the parchment a beautiful bright green so that you can

nim spangrün als vil du wilt und rib das gar wol mit essich und müsche dar under des grünen da mit die sekler leder verwent und disie zwei temperer under enander das es weder ze dik noch ze dünne si dar nach so nim das geweschen bermit und netz das bermit in der varwe ze beiden sitten und las es also ligen in der varwe ein nacht dar noch so swenke daz bermit in kalten Wasser und spanne das berment stark uff ein ram und las es wol truken werden darnach so nim luter virnies das usser mastikel gemachet sig und mit dem selben virnis das berment ze beiden sitten bis daz es glantz wirt darnach so setz es in eine heisse sunne und las das bermit wol truken werden dar nach so schnid das bermit glich us der ramen und mach drie stück oder 4 als breit als du es haben wilt und leg dis bermit in ein buch oder in ein presse das es schlecht[35] belibe.

Wellent ir violvarw tüchlin machen das ouch gar nütz ist zu vil dingen zu dem ersten sol man frü an dem morgen vor mittem tag gewinnen der grossen schönen roten blumen[36] als vil man wil und sol man die bletter alle abe brechen anders es verhende die varwe wenn man si alle ab gebrichet so sol man si stossen in einen reinen stein oder in einen mürsel und ringe den die varwe gar genot us und durch ein zwilchin tuch und enphahent die varwe in ein überlazurt kachlen und nement aber als gros aluns als ein haselnus ze bulver geriben uff einen stein und reret den alun in der varwe und rurent es wol under enander bis das der alun in die varwe zergangen si und denn nement aber rein wol geweschen linim tücher und tekent die wol in der varwe zu beiden sitten und das si ouch die varwe alle gar in sich nement und ouch nüt — trieffend und henkent ouch den die tücher uff an den wind und land si wol truken werden und trenkent die tücher zu dem andren mol aber in der varwe und lond si aber dar noch wol truken werden und nement schönen wol geverwten win wol uff ein mos und legent in den roten win ein lot luters gumis und das gumi lant einen halben tag ligen in den roten win zu weichen und zertribet das gumi gar wol under den roten win und netzent die geverwten tücher ze hindrest mit dem rothen win und des wines sol nüt me sin wand blos als vil das die tücher under uff an den wint und land si gar wol truken werden und tund si denn wol rein behalten in ein schindellad untz das man ir bedarf und so hast viol varw tüchlin var.

Wellent ir schön fin tüchlin blau var machen nach lamptschen sitten[37] damit man schön blau verwet und ouch garn und ist ouch gut zu vil dingen und blauen buchstaben und uff silber statz als ein fin blau gesmeltz. In der Zit acht tag nach phingsten so sol man an dem morgent frü uff stan so die sunne erst uff gat das maaden do si

see through it as you can through glass, take verdigris as much as you think you need and grind it well with vinegar, then mix it with the green which saddlers use to dye leather and mix these two well together so that the mixture is neither too thick nor too thin. Next take the washed parchment and dip it in the colour so that both sides get thoroughly wet, then leave it lying in the liquid overnight. After this, rinse the parchment in cold water and stretch it on a frame to dry thoroughly. Next take varnish made of mastic; paint it over both sides of the parchment till it looks quite shiny, and then place it in hot sunshine to let it dry thoroughly. Later cut the parchment out of the frame—cut it into three or four strips the size you require and lay these either in a book or in a press to keep them flat[35].

When you want to make a violet rag colour which is useful for many things, you must in the first place, manage one morning before midday to gather some of those beautiful large red[36] flowers —as many as you require—you must break off only the petals or the colour will be spoilt; when they have all been pulled off you must crush them in a clean stone vessel or in a mortar and wring the colour out thoroughly through a straining cloth and collect it into a glazed earthenware dish. Then take a piece of alum the size of a hazelnut, ground to powder on the slab and sprinkle it into the colour and stir it well together until the alum is quite dissolved. Then take well-washed linen rags and soak them in the colour so that they are thoroughly saturated and yet not wet enough to drip and then hang out these rags in the open air and leave them to dry. Now soak them again in the colour and once again leave them hanging up to dry. Next take some wine of a good red colour, at least a *mos* and put into it ½ oz. of pure gum arabic and let it steep in the red wine for half a day to soften; then stir it thoroughly in the wine and lastly soak the coloured rags in the red wine so that it is all sopped up. Keep turning them over in the air until they are quite dry and then store them in a drawer to keep them quite clean until you need them —and this is how you make a really good violet colour.

When you wish to make a lovely bright blue rag colour, according to the London[37] practice, with which you can dye yarn and which is also of use for many things such as letters in blue and serves for a transparent glaze over silver, you should proceed as follows: About a week after Whitsun, get up early in the morning, at sunrise so as to be able to get in time to where the flowers are growing. Then pick handfuls of these blue flowers—and this must be before midday because after that they are no good. You will need three or four persons to break the tops off into a clean pot and as soon as that is

do di blumen stant und sol gewinnen — 17 — hant vol der blumen
die blauen vor dem mittem tage wan nach dem mittem tag sint si
nüt gut und und süllen 3 monschen oder 4 oben ab brechen in ein
rein bekin oder in ein schön Kar und so das geschicht so soll man die
blumen stossen in einen reinen mürsel stein gar wol untz das die
blumen ze mus werdent und nas genug und do noch so nement ein
rein zwilchin tuch und netzent das vorhin enwenig mit Wasser und
ringent das wasser wider us dem tuche und legent das genetzet tuch
in die gestossenen blumen und als gros als ein gans eij[38] und ringent
das blau safft genot us mit 2 reinen seken[39] untz nüt me varwe dar
us gange und emphahent die varwen in ein rein überlazurt kacheln
und nement aber me der gestossen blumen in das tuch und ringentz
aber us als vor und tund die varwe alle ze samme in ein rein geschirre
und wenne das alles geschicht so schetz ist der varwe ein halbe mos
oder etzwas minder so nement ein settit aluns und ouch ein settit sal
armoniac und stossent die 2 ze bulver und rerent das bulver in die
varwe untz das es alles wol zergangen ist in der varwe und teilent denn
die varwe in zwen teil gelich in zwei rein geschirr also das in einem
geschirr glich als vil si als in dem andren und nement rein alti
tücher linin die vorhin gar wol gebuchet[40] und wiss geweschen sint
und stossent die tücher in die varwe und windet si das die tucher dur
nas werdent das si zu beiden sitten wol und gelich gerverwt sint und
ouch die varw gar in gangen si und die tücher nüt entriffent und so
henkent die geverwten tücher uff an den wind an ein seil oder an
einen steken und land si als wol troken werden und stossent denn
die selben geverwten tücher noch einist in die andern varwe und das
si die varwe an sich gewinnent gar das der varwe nüt me belibe und
henkent denn die geverwten tücher aber uff an den wint und land si
hangen untz das si gar wol trochen werdent und also sigent si —
zwurent geverwet und do noch so heissent aber an dem morgent
blumen gewinnen vor mittem tag als vor so vil das die tücher noch
einist mügent nas werdent und tund den hindresten blumen mit
stosse und mit us truken als den vordresten und tund 1 lot luters
gumis in die hindresten varwe aber das gumi sol vorhin in enwenig
wassers geweichet sin und mit einem finger wol zertriben sin und
denn sol man das gumi giessen in die dritte hindresten varwe und das
gumi gar wol ruren in die varwe und sol die geverwten tücher zu dem
dritten mol in die varwe stossen das si aber die varwe alle an sich
nement das die varwe nüt me si und die tücher ze beiden sitten wol
geverwt sin mit der hindresten varwe und denne so sint die tücher wol
geverwt und hand ouch varwe genug und blibent also lang zit schön
und ouch stette und fin sol si aber uff henken an dem wint zwene tage

done, they must be well crushed in a mortar till the flowers are reduced to a juicy mash. After this, take a clean straining cloth, first moistening it in a little water and, wringing it out again, lay it on the crushed flowers taking up as much of the mash as would equal a goose[38] egg and wring out the blue juice, using two clean sticks[39] to wring it out thoroughly, until no more liquid comes out. The colour should be collected in a clean glazed earthenware vessel, more of the crushed flowers being put into the cloth and wrung out again as before. When the colour has all been collected into a clean vessel it is ready to be stored.

If the colour were half a pint or rather less, take one *settit* of alum and the same quantity of sal-ammoniac and grind the two to powder and sprinkle this into the liquid until it has dissolved. Now divide the colour into two equal quantities each one in a clean vessel so that there is exactly half in each. Then take some clean pieces of old linen that have been well bleached[40] and washed white and steep the rags in the colour. Then turn them over so that they get thoroughly saturated and are evenly coloured on both sides; the colour quite soaked up yet the rags not dripping. Then taking them out carefully, hang them up in the open air on a line or on a clothes-horse and leave them to dry. Next steep these same coloured rags in the second lot of colour, until they soak it all up, and no liquid remains. Then hang them up once again in the open air and leave them until they are quite dry and in this way they will be double dyed. Then the next morning hurry off once more to fetch more flowers before midday so that the rags may be dipped once again. Treat these last flowers by crushing and straining in the same way as before, putting ½ oz. of clear gum in the last lot of colour. Remember that the gum should be softened first in a little water and well stirred round with the finger and then one must pour the gum into this third and last lot of colour. Then you must dip the rags in the colour so that they soak it all up and there is not a drop left, the rags being well coloured on both sides. Now at last they will be coloured sufficiently and will keep their beauty and brightness without fading. They must be hung up again for forty-eight hours till they are quite dry and then they are ready for use. The blue rags must be wrapped in paper and be laid in a clean wooden box and must then be kept on some high shelf where it smells sweet[41] and clean and where the colour will not be affected by mould. If the rags are kept in this way, they will remain fresh and lovely for as long as twenty years without fading. In Paris and in London[42] this colour is called blue for missals[43], but here in this country rag blue and it is a good and valuable colour.

und nacht untz das si gar wol truken werdent und also sint si wol
bereit und die blauen tücher sol man in pappir winden und sol sie
legen in ein rein schindellad und sol die laden setzen u. behalten
enboruff einem schafft do mit vil rothes aber ander besser gesmak[41] si
und also man man sie 20 jar wol behalten frisch und schon das ir
varwe niemer verwanlet und diese varwe heisset ze paris und ze
lampten[42] vor misal[43] und hie im land tüchlin blau und ist liep und
wert.

Wiltu blauen faden verwen nim heidelber und truk das saff dar us
und tu es in ein suber schüssel und las es enwenig wallen und nim
den zu einer mess safftes ein halb ei gros alun und als vil kupher
foulen und ouch als vil weid eschen oder enwenig me und zerstos die
und den alant wol und wirft es denne alles in das safft und güss
enwenig essichs darzu und rur es wol und tu den faden dar in und las
in wol erwallen so gewinst du schönen und fast habenden faden wiltu
aber das er liecht werde so nim der kupher fölen dester me.

Wiltu schwartz tinten zu brieffen geschriffte nim gallas romanas
zween teil das dritteil vitrioli iöni das ist ougstein das vierde teil
gumi arab. wiltu aber die tinten über all mal swartz machen so nim
das funfte teil nas schürfen dis sol man alles ze bulver klein stossen
und sol das bulver in einen hafen tun und lourinden wasser dar zu
das sol man lan sieden als lang als vische und sol man es nüt lassen
überlouffen und tu dar zu ein gleslin vol essichs und hab die tinten
von dem für und rur si untz das si kalt werde und las ein hut dar uber
wachsen so schimelt si nüt fürbas hie merki ist die vorgn materie
1 phunt gewesen so hourt dis vorgn lourinden wassers 1 vierling dar
zu Item zu einem halben phunt mosse wiltu machen tinten von
substancie.[44] Nim substancie als gros als zwei hennen eiger und $\frac{1}{2}$
mos wines und 1 zekel bermentz und süd das in einem nüwen hafen
untz das es wol zergangen si und nim denn atrament als gros als ein
boun nus und brounne das in einem füre und rib es denn in einer
schüssel und schüt es denn in die tinten und rur es under enander
und achte daz es siede und nüt übergange so si denne gesüdet so
rur untz das si kalt wirt so wirt si ze mol gut.

Wiltu gut blaw varw machen nim der blumen von dem Korn du
weisst wol wenn und derre die sentfteklich und rib es denne mit guten
wine und las es denn trukne und nim den enwenig ganffer und halb
als vil salis armon. und rib es ouch dar under so hastu uff silber oder
wa du wilt gut blau als fin lazur und tp. es denn mit gumi oder mit
wasser von eiger clor.

When you wish to dye thread blue, take bilberries, and press out the juice and put it in a clean vessel and let it cook for a short time and take one measure[?] of juice, half an egg shell of alum and the same amount of copper filings and also of wood ashes or a little more and pound them well together with the alum and then throw it all into the juice, pouring a little vinegar on it and stirring it well round —then immerse the thread and let it cook thoroughly. In this way you will have made fine permanently dyed thread. If however, you want it to be a lighter shade, you must add more copper filings.

If you want black ink, for writing letters, take two parts oak apples, one part vitriol of iron and the fourth part gum arabic. If you wish the ink to be exceptionally black, add one fifth part more of liquid vitriol. All these must be ground up fine into powder and this must be put in a cooking pot with some *lourinden* water with it. This must be allowed to cook as long as you would boil fish and it must not be allowed to boil over. Add to it a small glass of vinegar and take the ink from off the fire and stir it until it is cold, for if you let a skin form on it, it will be no good. Note that if the foregoing materials mount up to one pound, a quarter of a pint of *lourinden* water will be sufficient, but if to only half a pound, less in proportion. If you want to make ink from oak apples[44], take as much of the cores (or kernels) as would equal two hens eggs and $\frac{1}{2}$ *mos* of wine and a *zekel* of parchment clippings and boil them up in a glazed pot till well dissolved, then take the size of a walnut of *atramentum* and heat this over the fire, crush it in a bowl and throw it into the ink and stir it together, taking care that it cooks slowly and does not boil over. When it is cooked enough, go on stirring it until it is cold and it will be good for painting.

If you want to make a good blue, take cornflowers, you will know the season, and dry them carefully and mix them with some good wine and let them dry. Then take a little camphor and half as much sal-ammoniac and grind it all together. This makes a good bright blue for transparent glazing over silver or over anything else you want it for. It must be tempered with gum arabic or with liquid glaire.

A. Dis buchlin lert wie man all varwen tempieren sol ze molen und ouch ze florieren nach lampenschen sitten[45] und ouch von allen durschinigen varwen rot blau[46] und wie man durschinig bermit sol machen luter als ein glas. Es lert ouch machen drier leige gold grunde und lert ouch drier leige virnis machen und zu dem ersten 2 wasser damit man alle varwe tempiereren mag und ist dis das erst gumi wasser.

Wiltu machen zwei[47] edli guti wasser domit man all varwen schön und vin tempiereren mag so nim zu dem ersten zwei teil gumi arab. und das dritteil gumi cerusa. und leg disie zwei gumi in ein schön schüsseln und güs schön Wasser oben über das gumi das das Wasser über das gumi gang eines vingers hoch und las das also stan ze weichen wol uff einen halben tag so ist das gumi in dem wasser wol weich werden un so zertrib die gumi mit einem finger wol under das es wol under enander gemischet si und getempt und tu ein klein nuschal vol honges in das wasser und ein eiger schal vol essichs und dises sol man gar wol under enander triben und müschen und sige das wasser durch ein rein tüchlin und tu dis wasser in ein rein glas behalten bis das man sin bedarff die wasser sol sin in der diki als öli so ist im recht gut und slecht.

hic depinge colores

Ze vachent an die durschinigen varwen wie man die bereiten sol und zu dem ersten wie man zweier ley grün machen sol. Nim vin spangrün als vil du wilt und rib das in einen stein gar wol mit essich und rib als gros winsteines dar under als ein erwis und ouch drie troph eiger totter oder so vil honges und tp. das alles wol under enander mit itelm essich weder ze dik noch ze dünne und tu das in ein Küphrin geschir und leg luter gumi arab. dar in als ein halb bönus und las das in der grünen varwe wol weich werden und zertrib das gumi wol under dir grünen varwe so hast du edel vin duschinig grün varwe. Wiltu aber der selben varwen ein teil verwandelen zu schöner lougme varwe so müsch zwei blümelin saffrantz oder zwei under die grünen varwe so wirt es schön und loup var grüne.

This [part of the] book teaches how one should prepare all colours both for painting and for illuminating, according to the London[45] practice and also all about transparent colours, both warm and cold[46] and how to make parchment as transparent and clear as glass.

It also teaches how to make three kinds of gold size and three kinds of varnish and to start with, two different mediums with which all colours can be tempered, and the first of these is a gum medium.

If you wish to make two[47] really good mediums with which all colours may be tempered to make them beautifully bright, take, to start with, two parts gum arabic and one part cherry gum, and put these two gums in a clear bowl and pour over them pure water to cover the gum by a finger's breadth. Leave this to soften for about half a day. When the gum is well softened in the water, stir it well round with the finger till it is thoroughly mixed together. Then put a small potful of honey in this mixture and half an egg shell of vinegar. Stir this all well together to amalgamate the mixture and strain it through a clean cloth. Then pour it into a clean glass bottle and keep till required. This medium if properly prepared should be of the consistency of a thin oil.

hic depinge colores

Let us start with the transparent colours and how to prepare them, and first of all with the way to make two kinds of green. Take good quality verdigris, as much as you require, and grind it thoroughly on the slab with vinegar and grind as much as the size of a pea of tartrate of potash and also 3 drops of egg-yolk or the same amount of honey and mix it all together with this same vinegar, neither too thick nor too thin. Put it in a copper vessel and add pure gum arabic, in quantity half a walnut, and let it soak in the green colour until it is thoroughly soft. Mix the gum until it is quite incorporated, and you will have a wonderfully bright transparent green. Again, if you wish to alter this to more of a leaf-green, mix two or three flowers of saffron with it and it will make a lovely transparent leaf-green colour.

Wiltu schön vin durschinig rot machen das leicht und satt si so
nim persilien holtz ein halb lot das vorhin klein geschaben si und leg
das in ein rein glasiert geschirr und nim enwenig luter lougen und
mach die lougen heis bi dem für und güs die lougen heis über das
persilien holtz und tu ouch enwenig harnes dar in und rur das holtz
alles under enander und nim als gros aluns als ein gros haselnus und
rib das zinober[48] und tu das selbe bulver in die lougen zu dem holt
und rur es alles wol under enander — so — ziechet die louge und der
harne und der alun die rötin us dem holtz die es geleisten mag
und wirt die lougen schön fin rot als ein schöner roter rose.

Dis varwe sol man behalten rein bedeket untz man ir bedarff
wenn du nu diser varwe wellest bruchen ze schriben oder ze malen so
güs die roten varwen in ein rein nuschale und leg das gumi in die
varwe und lasse es in der varwe zer gan und rur es under enander mit
einem finger und strich die varwe uff gelich mit einem bensel so wirt
die varwe schön und vin durschinig rosuar rot und ouch glantz und
dise rote varwe mag man ouch us der vedren schriben. Wiltu nu die
selben roten varwe wandelen zu schöner purpur varwe so überstrich
die rote varwe mit einem bensel mit starkem lougen oder mit kalk
wasser oder mit gebrenten wine so verwandelet sich die rote varwe
bald zu schöner purpur die ist gar noch violvarw un stat under allen
andren varwen zierlich und wol.

Wiltu schön violvarw machen so nim lamptschen endich[49] und
zwürent als vil prisilien roter varwe und müsche dar under ein
nuschal vol starker lougen oder kalk wasser und rur das under
enander und leg luter gumi in die varwe und wo du das uff wis ding
strichest das wirt schön glantz.

Wiltu aber ein ander violvarw machen so nim violvarw tüchlin
varwe und leg des tüchlins als vil du wilt in ein nuschal und güs
enwenig gumi wassers oder clares dar über und netz es wol und lasse
es enwenig weich werden und ring denn die varwe genot us
weder ze dik noch ze dünne und schrib oder mol oder florier do mit.

Wiltu schön purpur machen zu gewendelin oder zu veldunge in
buchstaben oder zu blumen und zu dingen so nim liecht lazur und
müsch dar under enwenig röselin varwe und ouch enwenig bliwis
und tp. das wol under enander weder ze dik noch ze dünne als die
andren varwen so hast du schön purpur.

Hie wil ich leren wie man gelwe durschinig varwe tempiereren sol
nim saffrantz als vil du wilt und bind den in ein rein linin tuchlin und
leg das in ein schön nuschalen und güs gumi wasser dar under und
las es ein wenig weich werden in dem gumi wasser und truke denne
die varwen us und ist die varwe ze stark und ze rot so tu me wassers

44

If you want to make a beautiful, bright transparent red, light yet rich, take brazil wood ($\frac{1}{4}$ oz.) that has been pared into shavings and put it in a clean glazed vessel and take a little pure lye and make it hot and pour it over the brazil wood. Add a little urine and stir all together, then take as much alum as a big hazel-nut and grind it to powder[48] and put it into the lye with the brazil wood and stir well together. In this way, the lye, urine and alum together draw out every bit of the red stain from the wood and the liquid becomes the colour of a lovely red rose.

This colour must be kept well covered till required. When you want to use it, either for writing or painting, pour it into a clean pot and add some gum arabic to it and let this dissolve; stir it with the finger and apply it evenly with a brush and thus you will have a lovely, bright transparent rosy red. It can also be used for writing with a quill. If you want to make this red turn a good purple, lay a coat with a brush on the red either of strong lye, lime water or hot wine; in this way the colour soon changes to a rich purple, quite different from a true violet and blends well with any other colour.

If you want to make a good violet colour, take some London[49] indigo and twice as much brazil red and add to this a pot full of strong lye or lime-water and stir together. Then put pure gum arabic in the colour and wherever you paint it over anything white, it will show up brilliantly.

If you want to make another kind of violet, put as much as you require of your violet rag colour in a paint-pot and pour gum-water or liquid glaire over it, till it softens a little and then wring out the colour thoroughly. This should be neither too thick nor too thin; and you can both write and paint and also flourish with it.

It you want to make a lovely purple for drapery or for laying in the flat tints of letters, of flowers, or of other things, take light blue azurite and mix it with a little rose colour and a little lead white. Temper it well, neither too thick nor too thin like the other colours and you will have a good purple.

Now I will teach you how to prepare transparent yellow. Take some saffron, as much as you require, and wrap it in a little piece of clean linen. Put this in a paint pot and pour gum water on it and let it soften a little in this. Then wring the colour out. If you find the colour too strong and too deep, put a little more gum water with it and mix it round with a finger till the yellow becomes lighter. However, when you require a deep yellow, do not add any more gum water to it and see that there is a good difference between these two shades of yellow. Thus you will have transparent yellow in both a deep and a

von gumi dar in und zertrib es under enander mit einem finger bis das die gelwe varwe lichter wirt und doch wiltu die gelwe varwe gerne also satt han so tu nüt me gumi wassers dar in und luog wie dir die varwe gevalle an setti und an der liechti und las si also beliben unvermischz so hast du durschinig gel varwe satt liecht noch allen dinnen willen.

Wiltu aber ein schön durschinig gel varwe machen uff alle wissi ding die als schön sint als oppriment so nim der rinden von erbsellen holtze und tu si in ein rein hefelin und güs schön luter wasser daran und las das wol den dritteil insieden und behalt die varwe in ein rein glas untz du ir bedarfft so diese varwe wilt bruchen so güs enwenig us dem glas in ein nuschal und leg enwenig luters gumis dar in und las in der varwe zer gan und rur die varwe under enander mit einem finger und wo uff die varwe wirt gestrichen oder geschriben so ist si schön durschinig liecht gel varwe.

Wiltu erbstel gel varwe machen so nim zu dem ersten (*es fehlt der Rest in dem Manuscript*).

Jetzt wirt gesagt wie man durschinig harvarwe[50] machen sol jugen lüten.

Zu dem ersten wie man sol zinober tpiereren ze schriben und ouch ze florieren so nim zinober als vil du wilt der vorhin wol geriben si und leg den zinober uff einen reinen rib stein und güs des vorgñ gumi wassers uff den stein uff die varwe das si wol us und tu dri troph eiger tuttern dar under und rib es enwenig under enander und tus von dem stein in ein rein horn ob du de mit wilt schriben ist es ze dik so güs me eiger clor dar an und rur die rote tinten wol under enander als dik man die fedren oder den bensel in die roten varwe tunket so wirt die tinte gelich schön rot getempt wenn man aber die tint nüt vorhin ruret so wallet die varwe ze boden und wirt die geschrift nüt schön rot als obe man die varwe het wol under enander wol geruret.

Wiltu aber die ruberik über die mass röter und viner und glantzer so nim in der appitegen als gros aleo opaticum als ein bone und tu das in die rote tinte disi kunst ist hennlich.

Wiltu schön vin blau tinten tpier. ze schriben und ouch ze malen so nim liecht blau lazur[51] 1 lot oder $\frac{1}{2}$ oder minder oder me und leg das lazur in ein gros nuschal und güs des vorgñ gumi wassers enwenig daran und rur es mit einem finger gar wol under enander und güs aber me gumi wassers daran und leg als gros wisser mirren dar in als ein bon oder als vil gumi tragantum und las das in der blauen varwe

light tone, for whatever purpose you require.

Again if you want to make a lovely transparent yellow glaze over white that is as good as orpiment, take the bark of Berberis wood and put it in a clean saucepan, and adding clear water, let it boil till it reduces to two-thirds. Keep the colour in a clean glass bottle and when you want to use it, pour a small quantity into a paint-pot and add a little pure gum arabic to it letting it dissolve. Stir the colour well round with the finger and wherever you paint or write with it, it gives a lovely transparent pale yellow.

If you want to make a beautiful Berberis yellow [the rest of the sentence is missing in the manuscript].

Now we will tell you how to make a transparent colour for the hair[50] of young persons.

First of all this is how one should temper vermilion for writing and flourishing. Take vermilion as much as is required that has first been well ground; put it on a clean grinding slab and pour the usual gum water over it till it is well saturated? then add three drops of egg-yolk and grind it together a little. Next take it from the slab and put it in a clean ink-pot. If it is too thick when you want to write with it, dilute it with liquid glaire, stirring the red ink thoroughly. For if you stir the liquid well round with a pen or brush, your ink will be evenly mixed with the red, whereas if you do not stir it well the colour will sink to the bottom of the pot and your writing will not be such a good red as if it had been well stirred up.

It may happen that you wish to make a ruberic stand out particularly well and show up more brightly coloured than usual, in which case take half a teaspoonful of *aleo opaticum* bought at the chemists and add it to the red colour—but this is a secret 'wrinkle.'

If you want to prepare a lovely bright blue ink for writing or illuminating, take light blue azurite[51], $\frac{1}{2}$ an ounce or so, and put it in a large paint-pot and pour on a little of the usual gum water. Stir it well together with the finger, then add a little more gum water, and the size of a bean of white myrrh or the same amount of gum tragacanth and let it soften by soaking in the blue; then stir it well together and put it in an ink-pot and when you want to write with it, be sure

wol weich werden und zertrib es denn wol under enander und tu es in das horn ob du do mit wilt schriben und rure es wol under enander und tunke ein fedren dar in und gat si schön und gern us der fedren so ist ir recht.

Safft grün. Item in dem herbst so der win zittig ist so vindet man ber[52] veil wechelber oder tinten ber. Der beren nim wie vil du wilt einen becher vol oder me und solt die ber zer truken und zerbrechen in einem reinen geschirre und das safft wol us den beren ringen dur ein rein stark linin tuch und tu das safft in ein reinen nüwen hafen und güs wol uff ein halb mos wassers dar in und las das erwallen ane routh[53] und wenne es wol erwallen ist so tu zwei lot aluns in die varwe und las erwallen mit dem alun und las denn die varwe wol kalt werden und güs die varwe in ein lindes blottern[54] uff an den wint so wirt die varwe hert und düre in der blottern und ouch truken genug in einem monot und wirt ze glicherwise als substancie[55] do man tinten us südet und also mag man die varwe trothen und hert behalten wie lang man wil das dise varwe krafft niemer verlürt in disen weg und wenn man diser varwe bruchen wil zu schreiwen oder zu andren dingen als do vor ist geseit so nim das gumi darin und strich das über das har so wirt es schon licht krum har varwe.

Wiltu aber brun har varwe zu iungen lüten so nim gelutertes ruswasser und leg gumi dar in und das[56] uber das har so wirt es schön licht brun har varwe.

Wiltu aber es noch brüner so strich die varwe noch einist an wiltu aber hor var so misch persilien rot under enander und mache das glantz mit gumi das wirt schön rot har varwe.

Wiltu aber ein ander frömde har varwe so nim 2 teil rusvarw und das dritteil persilien varw oder violvarw tüchlin varw und ouch enwenig safft grüns dar under und tp. das alles under enander und mach das glantz mit gumi das wirt gar ein froumde har varwe. Wiltu denn grau har varw machen zu alten luten so nim gar liecht blau har varwe[57] und tp. die gar stark mit gumi wasser daz si glantz werde und strich die varwe luter und dünner aber das hor so ist grau har varwe schön durschinig und ouch glantz und dis sint die durschinigen varwen alle gar und nüt me. Wiltu gelütert rus machen so nim des klebringen ruses knolle als vil du wilt und leg die in lougen und las die sieden das dritteil und las den horn also stan bedeket so fallent die feces davon alle ze boden und ist das oberste wasser schön vin har varwe war uff mans strichz und wenn du derselben varwen wilt bruchen so güs der varwen us dem hafen wie vil du wilt und tu gumi dar in das die varwe glantz werde und strich si war uff du wilt oder schetwe domit gewand oder stein gebirge wenn sü ist gut zu vil

to stir it well again and dip the pen in it and, if it flows well and easily, this means it is of the right consistency.

Sap Green. In the autumn, at the wine-making season, one finds various kinds of berries[52], such as violet, buckthorn and base broom and taking a bucket-full or more of one of these crush and bruise them in a clean bowl. Press the juice through a strong linen cloth and put it in a clean glazed vessel and pour over about $\frac{1}{2}$ mos of water and let it boil continuously[53]. When it is well cooked, add an ounce of alum to the colour and let it cook together. Afterwards let this get quite cold and pour the liquid into an ox bladder[54] and hang it up in the air till the colour becomes hard and dry, and in a month's time it will be just dry enough, the same consistency as the cores[55] of oak apples which you boil down to make ink, and if it is prepared in this way you can keep this colour in a dry state as long as you wish and it never loses its strength. When you want to use it for writing or for anything else add gum to it, as I showed you before and if you paint it over hair it will make a lovely light brown hair colour.

If you want to make another brown hair colour for a young person, take well prepared liquid bistre and put some gum arabic in it and paint[56] it over the hair in order to make it a nice light brown hair colour.

If you wish to make this darker, give another coat of the same colour. If on the other hand, you want a rather red hair colour, mix a little brazil wood red with it and make it lustrous with gum arabic. This will be a good colour for red hair.

If you want an unusual colour for hair, take two parts of bistre and the third of brazil wood red or of violet rag-colour, with also a little sap green in it, and mix all together and brighten it with gum and this will make a most unusual hair colour. If you want to make grey hair for an old person, take very light blue[57] and temper it strongly with gum arabic to make it very shiny. Then using it pure, paint it thinly over the hair. In this way grey hair can look pleasantly transparent and lustrous. These are all the transparent colours—there are no others.

If you want to prepare and refine bistre, take sticky lumps of soot, as many as you require and put them in lye and let them boil till reduced by one third and keep the pot covered. In this way, the solid part falls to the bottom and the liquid on top becomes a beautiful bright colour for hair.

When you want to use it, pour the colour out of the vessel, as much as you require, that is, and add gum water to make it shiny. Lay the colour in a flat wash wherever you wish or use it for shading draperies

dingen an ze strichen und ze menger ley schetwen.

Wer grün und gel under enander mischet das wirt loub var liecht grüne varwe dar uff man sol schetwen mit endich. Nim 2 teil persilien varwe oder paris rot und müsch darunder enwenig bliwis und gar enwenig minien oder zinobers und tp. das under enander mit gumi wasser und strich das an zu gewande und dar uff sol man schetwen mit paris rot oder mit sattem lazur oder mit tuchlin blau.

Wiltu liecht rouselin varw machen zu gewande oder zu blumen und zu rosen so nim persilien als vil du wilt und müsche dar under minder den das dritteil bliwis und daruff sol man schetwen mit paris rot oder mit endich oder mit tüchli blo. Nim liecht blau und halb als vil rouselin varwe und enwenig öliwis[58] und tp. das alles wol under enander mit gumi wasser daruff sol man schetwen mit paris rot oder mit sattem roselin oder mit endich oder mit tüchli blaue oder mit violvar tüchel. Item nim liecht blau lazur und müsche dar under violvar tüchel und enwenig bliwis und daruff sol man schetwen mit endich oder mit heildelber safft varw uff liecht blaue varwe schetwen mit endich oder mit tüchli blo oder mit tüchel uff satt blau sol man schetwen mit endich oder mit sattem paris rot.

Wiltu schön gold blumen machen. Item nim zwei teil geriben opiment und müsche under den den dritteil schöner minien dar under und tp. das als die andren varwen mit paris rot oder mit geluterten rus getempt. uff itel liecht gelwe varwe mag man schetwen mit satten saffran und das stat ouch wol zu gewande. Item nim zwei teil schönes vergers und minder den das dritteil schöne minie und tp. das als die andren varwen und schetwe dar uff mit gelütertem rus oder mit paris rot.

Wiltu schön grün varwe machen zu gewande so nim lazur eschen und tp. das mit saff grün ist es gesatte so müsch bliwis oder geriben criden dar under und tp. das als die andern varwe das ist liecht grun und dar uff sol man schetwen mit saff grün. Wiltu aber ein ander viner varwe machen grüner so nim gar schöner liecht blau lazur 2 teil und müsche minder den das dritteil bliwis dar under und güs das in saff grün das es weder ze dik noch ze dünne si und strich das an zu gewande oder zu boumen oder zu grase oder zu gebirge und dar uff sol man schetwen mit safft grün oder mit persil oder mit satter roselin varwe. Item wiltu aber ein schön grün machen zu gewande und zu boume und zu grase und zu gebirge nim enwenig us dem blatern und lege si in ein rein geschir und güs luter wasser dar über und las es enwenig weichen so zergat die varwe und hast schon vin saff grün und tp. das weder ze dik noch ze dünne so wirt recht zu allen dingen.

Wiltu violvar machen oder blau damit man ouch vil dinges zu

or rocks and mountains; for it is suitable both for laying flat washes and for various kinds of shading.

When green and yellow are mixed together they produce leaf green, that is a light green colour on which one must shade with indigo. Take two parts of either brazil wood red or Paris red and mix with it a little white lead and a very little red lead or else vermilion. Mix these together with gum water and use it for painting draperies and shade on it either with Paris red, pure azurite or with rag colour blue.

If you wish to make a light rose colour for drapery, for flowers or for rosy cheeks, you must take as much as you require of brazil red and mix with it less than a third (of the quantity) of lead white and on this you must shade either with Paris red, indigo or rag colour blue. Take light blue and half as much light rose colour and a little lead white[58] and temper it all well together with gum water. On this one must shade either with Paris red, pure rose colour, indigo or with blue or violet rag colour. Now take light blue azurite and mix with this violet rag colour and a little lead white and this must be shaded with indigo or with bilberry juice colour, on light blue shade with indigo or blue or violet rag colour; on deep blue shade with indigo or pure Paris red.

If you want to paint lovely golden yellow flowers then you must take two parts of well ground orpiment and mix with it a third part of good red lead and temper it in the same way as the other colours and shade it with Paris red or with refined bistre. On the yellow by itself shade with pure saffron and this is also suitable for draperies. Take two parts of good ochre and less than a third part of good red lead and temper them in the same way as the other colours and shade on this with refined bistre or with Paris red.

If you want to make a good green for drapery, take azurite ash and mix it with sap green, if this is too deep a colour add some white lead or ground chalk with it and temper it as you did the other colours. Now this is a light green, and you should shade on it with sap green. If, however, you want another brighter colour, greener than the first, take two parts very good light blue and mix with it less than the third of lead white and pour on it some sap green, making it neither too thick nor too thin and lay it in as your ground colour for draperies, trees, grass or mountains and shade on it either with sap green, brazil red or with pure rose colour. Then again, when you want to make a good green for draperies, trees, grass or mountains, take a little leaf green from a bladder and put it in a clean vessel and pour pure water on it and let it soften a little so that

bringet mit malen und mit schetwen und ist ouch gut mit ze verwen
menger leig uff leder und uff berment und garn linis und wullis und
side und zendal diese varwe behalt man ouch wol über ein iar frisch
und gut so sim heidelber so si gar wol zitig sind und stosse die ber
und zerbrich si gar wol und ring das safft gar wol us dur ein stark und
tu das saff in ein reinen nüwen hafen oder in ein kessel und las die
varwe erwallen und tu ouch ı lot aluns dar in oder ander halb lot zu
dem meisten und also ist dise varwe wol bereit zu behalten über iar
das man ir bedarff ze verwen oder zu andren dingen als da vor ist
geseit und also ist es schön violvar.

Wiltu si aber blau haben so nim dragantum oder Kuppfer wasser
oder alunen viridum und ist als eis und des vorḡn steines rib und tu
sin ein lot oder me darin so wirt es schön blau und wenn du garn und
linin tuch wilt verwen so nim der varwen als vil du ir berdarfft ze
verwen und tu ein löffel vol oulis in die varwe und sol das öli gar wol
zertriben mit einem löfel untz das öli wol gemischet wirt under die
varwe[59] und mach die varwe siedendig heis und tu den die varwe in
die varwe das das garn wol genetzt werde und so enphat es die varwe
wol und gat nüt me abe und also tu man ouch allen varwen.

Nu han ich redelich und merkelichen wol gelert wie man alle
varwen tpieren sol noch Kriegeschem sitten mit zwein wassern und
wie man die varwen under enander machen sol und wa man uff ie die
varwe schetwen sol die gantze wahrheit.

Nun wil ich leren wie man alle varwen mit lin[60] tpiere sol uff holtz
oder uff muren oder uff tüchern. Und zu dem ersten wie man den lin
dar zu bereiten sol das er lange wert und nüt ful wirt und ouch nüt
übel smekent wirt. Nim bermit schaben und wesche die vorhin
schön mit Wasser und süde dar under ein lutern lim weder ze stark
noch ze krank und wenn der lim ze hant gesotten ist so tu ein schüssel
vol essichs darin und las das wol erwallen und tu in denn ab von dem
für und sige in durch ein tuch in ein schön geschirr und setz in do er
kül habe so belibet er lang frische und gut. Ist der lim gestanden als
ein galrein und was varwen du wilt tpier. so nim limes als vil du wilt
und ouch als vil wassers als des limes si und müsche den lim und das
wasser under enander und ouch vil[61] honges dar under und werme
das enwenig und zertrib das honig gar wol under den lim und domit
sol man alle varwen tpier. weder ze dik noch ze dünne als die andren
varwen von den ich vor han geseit und dis varwen mag man ouch alle
wol über strichen mit virnis so werdent si glantz und mag nien niemer
kein wasser noch regen geschaden das si ir varwe noch ir glantz nüt
verlierent.

Wie man alle ouli varwen t̄pierē sol. Nu wil ich ouch hie leren wie

the colour dissolves and you have lovely bright sap green and temper it neither too thick nor too thin and it will be right for anything.

When you want to make a violet colour or a blue which is much used for painting or shading, and which is also good for dyeing many things, such as leather, parchment and linen or woollen yarn, silk and gauze, which colour can be kept fresh for over a year, take bilberries when ripe, crush them and mash them up well and wring out the juice well through strong linen into a clean glazed earthenware pan or cauldron. Let the colour simmer and add $\frac{1}{2}$ oz. of alum to it or $\frac{3}{4}$ oz. at most. Made in this way, the colour can be kept for over a year and is in the right condition to be used for colouring or for other things as has been already shown and it is a good violet colour.

Again if you want to make this into a blue tint, take $\frac{1}{2}$ oz. or more of either tragacanth or copper filings or *alumen viridum* crystals, and having ground it as usual on the slab, add it to the violet and it will turn a good blue. When you wish to dye yarn or linen cloth, take as much as you will require to colour it well and put into the colour a spoonful of oil, stirring it well with a spoon until the oil is well incorporated with the colour; then make the dye boiling hot and immerse the yarn[59] in the colour so that it is quite saturated and takes up the colour well and is permanently dyed. And this is the proper way to dye with all colours.

By now I have conscientiously and categorically taught how all colours should be prepared according to the Byzantine[?] tradition with two mediums and how you mix the colours and how the shading is done on each colour and I have told you all there is to know.

Now I am going to teach you how all colours may be tempered with size[60] for putting on wood, on walls and on fabric. To begin with I will teach you how to prepare the size so that it will remain good for a long time, and will not smell bad. Take parchment clippings and first of all wash them well with water and make from them with water a clear size neither too strong nor too weak and as soon as it is cooked, put a saucerful of vinegar in it and mix it well and let it boil up again. Then take it off the fire and strain it through a cloth into a clean vessel and put it aside in a cool place. Treated in this way it will keep fresh for a long time. When the size has set to a jelly and you want to temper your colours with it, take an equal quantity of water and of size and mix them well together, add a very little[61] slightly warmed honey which should be well mixed round in the size; and with this medium one can temper all colours, neither too thick nor too thin, just like the other colours I have taught you about.

man alle varwen mit oli tpier. sol bas und meisterlich denn ander moler und zu dem ersten wie man das oli dar zu bereiten sol das es luter und clor werde und dester gern bald troken werde.

Wie man das öli[62] zu den farwen bereiten sol. Man sol nemen linsamen öli oder hanfsamen oli oder nus öli als vil man wil und leg dar in alt gebrent wis bein und ouch als vil bimses und las das in dem öli erwallen und wirf den schum oben abe von dem öli und setz es ab dem füre und las es wol erkülen und ist des ölis ein mos so leg zwei lot galicen stein[63] dar in in das öli und so zergat er in dem öli und wirt gar luter und ouch klar und dar nach so sige das öli durch ein rein lin tuchlin in ein rein bekin und setz das bekin mit dem öli an die sunne 4 tag so wirt das öli dik und ouch luter als ein schöner cristall und dis öli das troknet gar bald und macht alle varwe schön luter und ouch glantz und umb dis öli wüssent nüt alle moler und von der güti dis olis so heisset es oleum preciosum wand i lot ist wol eines schillinges wert und mit olin sol man alle varwen riben und ouch tpier. alle varwen in der diki riben und ouch tpier. als ein halber bri[64] der weder ze dik noch ze dünne si.

Dis sint die varwen die man mit öli tpieṝe. sol zu dem ersten zinober nimien[65] paris rot röselin rot liech blau lazur endich und ouch swertz opiment gel rüschelecht[66] verger antlitbrunrot spangrün endich grün und ouch bliwis. Dis sint die öli varwen und nüt me hie merke dis varwen sol man alle gar wol riben mit dem öli und ze[67] so sol man under ieglich varwe drie troph virnis riben und tu denn ie die varw sunder in ein rein geschirr und würke do mit was du wilt und wele varwe du wilt liechterhaben wenn si an ir selber sint darunder sol tu bliwis wol müschen so werdent die varwen liechter und uff die liechten varwen sol man mit den satten varwen schetwen und sol si mit bliwis verliechten und verhörwen da es sin bedarff under alle dise vorgn. varwe mag man enwenig wises wol gebrentes beines riben oder enwenig wisses galicen steines als gros als ein bone umb das die varwe gern und wol troken werdent.

Alle varwen lant sich under enander mischen en allen oppiment gel und rüsch gel die lident nüt spangrün noch nimien noch bliwis noch rus wo dise varwen enwenig keine under oppiment gel so verdürbe die gelwe varwe bald und aber endich oder liecht blau lazur lat sich wol müschen under das oppiment gel das es da von nüt verdurbet und wirt schön zu gewande zu grase und zu gebirge. Nim liecht blau und müsch dar under enwenig bliwis und schetwe dar uff mit endich oder mit paris rot. Nim liecht blau und halb als vil paris rot und noch minder bliwis und tp. das wol under enander und schetwe dar uff mit paris rot oder mit endich uff itelm zinober sol

These colours must all be covered with varnish which will make them shiny, after which treatment neither rain nor water can do them any harm and they will retain their gloss indefinitely.

How one should temper all oil colours. Now I will also teach you how one should temper colours with oil in a truly masterly manner, better than any other painters and to begin with, how to prepare the oil in order to make it purer and clearer and more siccative for painting.

How to Prepare Oil[62] for Colours. One must take linseed oil, hemp seed oil or old walnut oil, the required quantity and put in it white calcined bone dust and also the same amount of pumice powder. Let them simmer in the oil and skim off the scum, then remove it from the fire and allow it to cool thoroughly. If the quantity is one *mos*, put 1 oz. of zinc vitriol[63] into the oil. This will dissolve in the oil and cause it to turn much clearer and paler. After this, strain the oil through a clean linen cloth into a clean pipkin and leave this in the sun for four days and it will become thick and crystal clear. Now this oil is very quick drying and makes all colours lovely, clear and bright, and not all painters know about it; and on account of its excellence this oil is called *oleum preciosem*. ½ oz. of it costs at least one shilling. Colours must first be ground in the oil and then tempered with more oil, all pigments being ground and tempered to the consistency of a soft paste[64], neither too thick nor too thin.

These are the colours that can be tempered with oil. Firstly, vermilion, red[65] lead, Paris red, rose red (brazil wood), light blue azurite, indigo and also black; orpiment yellow, realgar[66], yellow ochre, burnt ochre, verdigris, green indigo and finally white lead. These are the oil colours and the only ones. Note that these colours must all be well ground with oil and[67] finally you must grind in three drops of varnish to every colour and put each one separately into a clean receptacle and use them for anything you require. And if you want to make any colour lighter than it is you must add some lead white, mixing it well together. These light colours must be shaded with their own pure colour and the lights must be further heightened with lead white as required. To all the above-mentioned colours you must add a little calcined bone dust or a little zinc vitriol—as much as a bean—in order to make the colour dry well.

The colours mentioned above can all be mixed with one another, with the exception of orpiment (both yellow and red) which do not mix with verdigris nor with red or white lead nor with bistre. For if the slightest touch of any of these colours were to be mixed

man schetwen mit paris rot oder mit satten rouselin und ouch minie. Item nim zinober und enwenig paris rot und noch minder bliwis das es weder ze liecht noch ze sat werde und schetwe dar uff mit zinober und di grund vesti schetwe mit paris rot. Item nim spangrün und müsch dar under enwenig bliwis weder ze liecht und ze satt und schetwe daruff mit sattem spangrün und die grund vesti mit endich.

Wiltu ein hüpsche varwe ze grünen[68] gewande so nim realgar das ist glich als rüsch gel und heisset ouch müsgift das sol man riben und tpieren. mit öli als die andren varwen und schetwe dar uff mit spangrün oder mit liecht blau oder mit endich oder mit zinober oder mit paris rot und schetwnge stand alle zierlich uff der einigen varwe. Item nim paris rot oder enwenig zinobers oder minie und müsche dar under bliwis das es wol liecht werde und schetwe daruff mit spangrün oder mit liecht blau oder mit endich. Item nim spangrün und halb als vil liecht blau und noch minder bliwis und müsch das alles wol under enander und ist es ze satt so tu me bliwis dar under und schetwe daruff mit endich oder mit paris rot oder mit satten violvar.

Item wil du ein schön libvar machen zu jungen lüten so nim enwenig zinobers ouch als vil minie und aller meist paris rot[69] und müsche dar under das merteil bliwis und tp. das alles wol under enander das die libvar weder ze rot noch ze bleich si und ist si ze rot so müsche me bliwis dar in untz das ir recht wirt daruff sol man setwen mit zinober do enwenig vergers und minie under si gemüschet und schetwe die antlit und hende und do das bild nakent si man sol di ougen und nasen uff strichen und die hende mit antlit brunrot do enwenig ruses under gemischet si und sterlini in die ougen sol man mit endich an strichen do enwenig spangrünes under gemischet si.

Aber ein ander libvarw zu braunen lüten so nim roten gebrennten verger und ein wenig minien und dristund als vil bliwis und tp. das wol under enander weder ze liecht noch ze satt und schetwe daruff mit brun rot do enwenig ruses si darunder getempt und die wangen sol man rüsimeren mit zinober do enwenig persil ⁻rot under gemischet si. Aber ein ander libvar zu alten lüten so nim minien und verger glich und enwenig lazur eschen und aller meist bliwis und tp. das alles wol under enander weder ze liecht noch ze satt und daruff sol man schetwen mit verger do enwenig brunrot under getempt̄ si und als mag man die schetwunge verwandlen das ein antlit anders wirt geschetwet denn das ander das si nüt alle glich sigent gestalt mit einer schetwunge.

Wiltu ein tötlich libvar machen zu crucifixen und zu erbermhertzigkeit so nim zwei teil lazur eschen und das dritteil vergers und enwenig minie und rib dar under das merteil bliwis weder ze satt

with orpiment, it would soon spoil the yellow. On the other hand indigo and light blue azurite can be mixed with orpiment without bad results and can be used with success for painting drapery, grass or mountains. Take light blue and mix with it a little lead white and shade on it with indigo or with Paris red. Take light blue and half as much Paris red, and still less white lead and mix it well together and shade on it either with Paris red or with indigo. Again on vermilion one must shade with Paris red or with pure colour and use this same shading also on red lead. Now take vermilion, plus a little Paris red and even less lead white so that it is neither too light nor too dark and shade on it with vermilion, then for the dark accents use Paris red. Again you can take verdigris and mix with it a little white lead to make it neither too light nor too dark and shade with pure verdigris and put in the dark accents with indigo.

If you want a beautiful grounding[68] colour for drapery, take realgar, which is the same as orpiment and is also called *musgift*. You must grind and temper this with oil like the other colours and shade on it with verdigris or with light blue or with indigo or with vermilion or Paris red. All these colours are suitable for shading with on the above colour. Take Paris red, a little vermilion or red lead and mix with it white lead so that it makes a very light tint and shade on it with verdigris or light blue or indigo. You can use verdigris and half as much light blue and still less white lead and mix these all together and if the colour is too strong add a little more lead and shade on it with indigo or Paris red or with pure violet colour.

If you want to make a good flesh colour for painting a young face, take a little vermilion, with an equal quantity of red lead and even more of Paris red[69] and mix in more than all of lead white and stir it all together and temper it so that the flesh colour is neither too white nor too red and if it is too red, mix in more white lead to make it right. You must shade on this with vermilion mixed with ochre and a little red lead. This applies to the face and hands and to any other places where the nude is to be painted. The eyes and nose as also the hands must be outlined with burnt ochre and black to which a little bistre has been added. The irises of the eyes must be put in with indigo to which a small quantity of verdigris has been added.

Again for the colouring of a bronzed complexion, you must take burnt ochre, a little red lead and three times as much of white lead and temper it all together, neither too light nor too dark and shade on it with red ochre into which a little bistre has been mixed and the cheeks must be coloured with vermilion to which a little brazil red has been added. Then again for the flesh colour of old people, take

57

noch ze liecht und schetwe dar uff mit verger do enwenig russ und endich under gemischet si oder mit itelm russ und strich die verger[70] und die nasen und die hende und was nakent si das strich us mit rus do enwenig endich under gemischet si oder enwenig brunrottes. Und dis sint die müschunge aller varwen und ouch die schetwunge alle gar die do zu den varwen von recht hörent.

Hie merkent alle dise vorgñ varwen die man verlüchten und ouch verhohen mit bliwis die gewant [?] die antlit wo es not durftig ist.

Item wiltu schön har varwe machen zu iungen lüten so nim itel verger mit öli getempt und müsch dar under enwenig bliwis und schetwe das har mit satten stein verger[71] und strich das har us mit brun rot do enwenig russ oder endich under getempt si. Item aber zu rote har varwe so nim verger und enwenig brun rot und noch minder bliwis und das schetwe mit itelm russ do enwenig brun rot under gemischet si und ouch das dar us[72] mit der selben varwe.

Wiltu graue har varwe machen so nim lazur eschen und müsche dar under enwenig endich und bliwis das es nüt ze satt werde und schetwe uff die har varwe mit russ do enwenig endich under si und strich die louke des hares us mit brunrot do russ unter gemischet si.

Wiltu aber ein rechti brun harvarwe machen so nim satt stein verger und müsch dar under enwenig rus und tp. das alles wol under enander und strich die louken us mit brunrot do swartz oder endich under gemischet si.

Wie man graue varwe und ouch ander gemenget varwe tpiren sol zu mümchen und zu andern geislichen lüten gewande. Item zu dem ersten nim swartz und enwenig endich under und müsch enwenig bliwis darunder das es wol liecht werde und daruff sol tu schetwen mit endich do enwenig swartzes under gemischet si und das wirt schön graue zu gewande und zu kappen.

Aber ein ander schön gemenget zu kappen und zu andren geislichen gewande so nim enwenig swartz und enwenig paris rot und enwenig endich und das merteil bliwis und das temp. wol under enander und schetwe dar uff mit endich do paris rot under gemischet si. Aber ein ander varwe so nim verger und enwenig endich und rus und das merteil bliwis und tp. das wol under enander und schetwe daruff mit iteln rus oder mit endich.

Nim verger und brunrot und enwenig paris rot und enwenig bliwis und tp. das wol under enander und schetwe dar uff mit paris rot do enwenig swartz und enwenig endich under getempert si.

Hie will ich leren wie man kurzenklich und ouch gar nützlich alle dinge vergülden und versilbern sol schön und ouch glantz und zu dem ersten wie man sol machen ein edel glas varwe dar uff man

equal quantities of red lead and ochre and a little azurite ash and even more lead white and mix them all together neither too light nor too dark; you must shade on it with a mixture of yellow and red ochre and you should always vary the shade colours from one face to another so that they are not all exactly the same.

Now when you have to depict a deathly pallor, as in the case of a crucifixion, which is intended to arouse feelings of compassion on the part of the beholder, you should proceed as follows: take two parts azurite ash and the third part ochre and a little red lead and more than all of white lead so that it becomes neither too dark nor too light and shade on it with ochre to which a little bistre and indigo have been added, or else shade with bistre alone. You should outline the eyes[70]—the nose and hands, and indeed all the nude with bistre and indigo or with burnt ochre. And these are the mixtures for all the colours and all the tints for shading which belong to them.

Here I should remark that the above-mentioned colours must have their lights and high-lights made by adding white lead, whether for draperies, or for faces and wherever light tints are required.

When you want to make a good colour for the hair of a young person, take the usual ochre tempered with oil, mix with it a little white lead and shade the hair with dark ochre[71], and outline with burnt ochre, into which a little bistre or indigo has been mixed. Again for red hair, take yellow ochre, a little burnt ochre and still less white lead and shade it with the same bistre to which a little burnt ochre has been added and outline[72] the hair with the same colour.

When you want to paint grey hair, take azurite pigment and mix with it a little indigo and white lead so that it is not too dark and then shade on the hair colour with bistre to which a little indigo has been added and outline the locks of hair with burnt ochre mixed with bistre.

If you want dark brown hair, take dark ochre and add a little bistre and temper it well together and outline the locks with burnt ochre to which either black or indigo has been added.

How to temper grey colours and also other neutral tints for monkish garb and for the robes of saints, etc.: First take black with a little indigo. Add a little white lead to lighten it sufficiently and then shade on it with indigo to which a little black has been added. This makes a nice grey for a habit and cowl.

Another good neutral shade suitable for cowls and for other clerical robes is made by taking a little black, a little Paris red and a little indigo with a lot of white lead. Mix these well together and

gold und silber leit troken schön vin und glantz und das das gold und das silber niemer ab gat weder von wasser noch von win und war uff du dise gold varwe strichest es sig isen stahel oder zin oder bli oder stein oder bein und andre alle gesmide oder tuch oder zendal̄ und sus ander alle dung do man dise varwe uff strichet.

Nim zwei teil vergers und das dritteil bol armonici und das vierde teil minien und rib das alles wol under enander uff einen rib stein mit lin öl und rib es ouch gar wol weder ze dik noch ze dünne als die andren öli varwen und rib ouch als gros wisses gebeines das gebrent si dar under als ein halb boun nus und ouch ein las kechelin vol der varwen und ouch als vil galicen steines als des beines ist gesin und wenn dis alles wol geriben ist so rib ze hindrest in die varwe ein halb nuschal vol virnis in die varwe und zertrib den virnis gar wol under die varwe und tu die varwe von dem stein gar in ein rein überlazurt kachlen und nim phlemlin von einer blattern und schnid das phlemlin sinwel das es recht kome über das kechelin und bestrich das phlemin zu einer sitten gar wol mit öli und das phlemlin leg oben an uff die varwe so hast du ein edel gut gold varwe daruff man gold und silber leit das es sinen schin und sin glantz niemer verlürt das phlemlin sol man alle wegen ander über die varwe legen so wachset kein hut über die gold varwe und also sol tu allen andern öli varwen tun so belibet si lang lind und werdent nüt balde hert.

Hie lere ich wie man uff dise goldvarwe vergülden sol zu dem ersten wiltu uff holtz oder uff tuch oder uff zendal̄ [73] vergülden so überstrich das holtz vorhin mit frischen lime zwürent oder dritund das das holtz werde[74] und tu den andren ouch also und wenn der lim truken wirt uff dem holtz oder uff dem tuch oder uff dem stein[75] so strich die goldvarw uber den lym mit einem weichen bürste bensel und strich die varwe glich und dünne uff und las die goldvarwe troken werden und ouch nüt ze gar und griff mit dem finger uff die varwe und ist die varwe troken und ouch glantz und hafftet dir der finger enwenig in der varwe so ist si in rechter mos ze vergülden so schnide din gold oder din silber und lege das ordentlich uff nach enandern wo die varwe si und truke das gold senfteklichen wider mit bounwollen uff die varwe untz das es alles gar verleit wirt mit golde oder mit silber und dar nach so ribe das gel über all mit wulle so vart das gold abe wo die varwe nüt enist. Und belibet das golde vast wo das gold hingestrichen ist. hie merk isen zin bli und alle andri herti[76] gesmide und bein und senliche herti ding die bedarfent nüt das man si vorhin mit lym überstriche wenn allem holtz und tuch aber uff steinen und uff muren die sol man vor mit öli trenken[77] eman die goldvar uff strichet und zu glicherwise als hie vor gelert ist also sol man

shade on this colour with indigo to which a little Paris red has been added. For another colour, take yellow ochre and a little indigo and bistre and still more white lead well tempered together, shading on it with the usual bistre or with indigo.

Take yellow and burnt ochre and a little Paris red and a little white lead, well mixed together and shade on it with Paris red to which a little black and a little indigo have been added.

Now I am going to teach you how to gild skilfully and expeditiously so that both gold and silver retain their brilliance. To start with I am going to tell you how to make a good gold size on which gold and silver leaf can be laid easily so that they dry without losing their lustre and from which neither water nor spirits can move them and this holds good for any surface on which this gold-size has been laid, be it iron, steel, tin or lead, stone, ivory or any wrought metalwork or woven material or terra cotta or any other such substance.

Take two parts of ochre and the third part of Armenian bole and the fourth part of red lead and grind all thoroughly together with linseed oil on the grinding slab, neither too thick nor too thin, just as you do with other oil colours. Then into a glassful of this colour grind as much as a half walnut of white calcined bone and an equal quantity of zinc vitriol and lastly when this is all well ground together add to the colour half a painter's pot of varnish, grinding it all well together. Collect the mixture from the slab putting it into a clean glazed jar. Then take a small piece from a bladder and cut this so that it comes right over the jar. Having rubbed one side of the skin well with oil, place it over the colour. This makes an excellent gold size on which gold and silver leaf can be laid without ever losing its sheen and brilliance. A piece of membrane must in any case always be placed immediately on top of the gold size so that no skin can form on top of this mordant and this holds good for all other oil colours to keep them liquid and prevent them becoming hard in a short time.

Now I am going to teach you how one should lay gold on this mordant. To start with, when you wish to gild on wood, on woven material or on terra cotta[73], first of all lay a coat of fresh [parchment], size two or three times so that the wood is thoroughly sized[74] and treat the other surfaces in the same way and when the size is dry on the wood or on the material or on the stone[75], paint the gold size on top of the size with a soft bristle brush and lay it on evenly and thinly and let it dry—but not absolutely—then touch it with the finger and if it is dry, yet looks shiny and feels slightly 'tacky' to your finger, it is in the right condition for gilding. Then cut your

ouch andri ding übergülden.

Hie wil ich leren gut virnis machen von drierley materien do usse ie der materie sonderlich ein gut edler virnis. Zu dem ersten nim des gemeinen virnis[78] glas ein phunt gewegen oder matik ein lib. und stosse der eins weders du wilt in einen reinen mürsel ze bulver und nim darzu drie phunt lin ölis oder hanf ölis oder alt nus öli und las das siden in einem reinen kesselin und schum das öli und hüt vor allen dingen das es nüt überlouffe und wen das erwallen ist und geschumet ist so rer das virnis bulver langsam nach enander in das heiss öli so zergat das bulver in dem olin und wenn das bulver gar zergangen ist so las den virnis siden gar senfteklich mit kleiner hitze und rur den virnis ie ze stunt das es nüt an brünne und wenne du sichest das der virnis gerottet dikelecht werden als zerlossen honig so nim ein troph. des virnis uff ein messer und las den troph enwenig kalt werden und griff mit einem finger uff den troph zuch den finger langsam uff und lat der virnis ein fedemlin mit dem finger uff ziechen so ist der virnis und ouch wol gesotten und lat er aber des fademes nüt so süde in bas untz er den faden wol gewinnet und sol in von dem füre und las in erkülen und sich denn den virnis dur ein stark linin tuchlin und ringe den virnis gar dur das tuch in ein rein glazürt hafen und behalt den virnis wol bedeket untz man sin bedarfft so hast du guten edelen lutern virnis den besten.

Wiltu aber ein andren guten virnis machen der luter und glantz ist als ein cristalle so nim gloriat in der appenteken 1 phunt und zwürent als vil ölis und las das ouch under enander sieden und tu im mit allen dingen als dem ersten und wenne er ouch einen faden gewinnet als der este so ist er ouch genug gesotten und ist ouch gerecht.

Nim alt hanf öli und mach es heis und schum es und und als vil[79] gebrentes beines eines alten Knorren und leg es dar in und süd es under enander und schum es recht wol und setz es zwen tag an ein sunnen. Wiltu in aber stark so nim 4 lot mastik und stoss es ze bulver oder 5 lot terpentuum und wenn das öli siedendig heisse si so soltu es dar in reren und rur es vast untz es gerat zech werden als ein faden also ist es bereit.

Wiltu durschinig bermit machen so nim ein mitel bermit hut und wesch si us luterm wasser oder us drin wassern untz das nüt me trüb davon gang und streiffe es denn durch die hend. Wiltu es denn grün haben so nim spangrün und rib es mit starkem essich und tu es in ein kuphrin geschirr wol tun und las es über nacht stan und seig das oben ab in ein ander geschirr das ouch kuphrin sin und tu das dristunt oder vierstund und nim denn has berment und leg es dar in ein klein wile und spann es denn an ein ramen und überstrich es mit

gold or silver and lay it carefully piece by piece wherever the gold size is and gently press down the gold on to the mordant by means of a piece of cotton, until the surface is completely covered with gold or silver. Afterwards, rub over the gilded surface with [lamb's] wool so that the gold comes away from those parts not covered with the gold-size, while adhering wherever the mordant has been laid. You should note here that iron, tin, lead and all other metal work and bone and other hard[76] substances do not require to be sized first as is the case with all wood and woven material while stone and walls (in addition to the size) require a coat[77] of oil before the gold-size is laid; all other substances should be gilded in the manner given above.

Now I will teach you how to make a good varnish from three different ingredients, each of which makes an uncommonly good varnish. To begin with, take 1 lb. of ordinary[78] varnish or 1 lb. of mastic and crush one or the other, whichever you wish, to powder in a mortar; to this 3 lbs. of linseed oil, hempseed oil or walnut oil must be added. Let the oil cook in a clean saucepan and skim it, taking care, above everything, that it does not boil over and when it is well cooked and all the foam has subsided, sprinkle the varnish powder slowly into the hot oil and the varnish will dissolve in it. When the powder has quite dissolved, let it simmer very gently on a low heat and stir continuously so that it does not burn and when you see that the varnish begins to thicken like liquid honey, take a drop of it up on a knife and let it cool, then put your finger on this drop and pull it slowly away and if the varnish draws up like a thread from the knife it means it is sufficiently cooked but if not continue cooking until the thread forms. When this has occurred, move it from the fire and let it cool; next strain the varnish thoroughly through a strong linen cloth into a clean glazed vessel. Keep this varnish well covered until you need it for use. You now have a very good clear varnish— the best possible.

If you want to make another good varnish, clear and brilliant as crystal, get 1 lb. of *gloriat* [of turpentine] from the chemists and twice as much oil and let it also cook together and do exactly the same as you did in the first recipe and as soon as you can draw up a thread as before, it is cooked enough and ready for use.

Take old hempseed oil and heat it and skim it and as much[79] as you require of calcined bone from a dried knuckle-bone and simmer together. Skim and then put it for two days in the sun. If you want it to be especially strong, take 2 ozs. of mastic and crush it to powder or 2½ ozs. *terebenthum* and when the oil is at boiling point you must

virnis so ist es bereit.

Wiltu spangrün machen oder tpier. so nim spangrün und rib denn den mit starkem essich und stoss es ze hüffelin und wenn es troken wirt so güs essich dar uff und das als dik untz das es satt genug werde.

Folgt ein artikel wie man pappir[80] machen sol noch besser den es an sim selber ist so dann wirt gesagt wie man alles gestein schön und glantz bolieren kann, wie man gestein weich machen kann das man si schnidet als keste, wie man einen agstein macht der alle ding tut als ein ander agstein, wie man ein andren klugen agstein sol machen, wie man schön fin helfenbein machen sol das glantz ist und das schöner und wisser ist wenn alles helfenbein.

Wiltu machen einen virnis do mit man alle ding virnisse sol die schön und glantz und fest belibent so nim 2 eiger clor oder 3 als vil du wilt und klopphe die clor wol und wirff den schum abe darnach ein lot gumi arab. das luter si und 1 lot gumi amigdular oder cerusar. das ist besser das luter dise 2 gumi sol man under enander riben und sol si legen in das vorgn; eiger clor und las es über nacht stan ze weich und zertrib es wol under enander und müsche dar under ein nuschal vol honges das sol man alles under enander wol zertriben und gehalt es in ein glas wol bedeken bis man sin bedarff was varwe darmit diesem virnis überstrichest die wir glantz schön luter ewenklich diser virnis sol in der diki sin als ein zerlossen honig und trukenet ouch balde.

Wiltu aber varwen temperieren so tu ein eiger schal vol essichs darunder und so es ze dike si müsche es mit luterm wasser und tu es in ein glas und sich es vorhin durch ein tuch.

Wiltu vin gold varwe[81] machen die von keiner füchtigkeit niemer ab gat und ist gut uff isen stachel uff zin uff bli uff alle ding so nim zwei teil vergers und das dritteil minien und das vierde teil bolum armenum und alls vil wisses gebrentes beines und als ein haselnus galicem steines die varwe sol man under enander riben mit linsat öli und 5 troph. virnis und truk das dur ein tüchlin gar wol und wenn du si uffstrichest so las si trothen werden das si enwenig füct si und sol den in der diki sin als honig dis ist die beste gold varwe die sin mag.

Ein ander gold varwe so nim aleo epaticum[82] und alea titoclonium beider glich als vil du wilt und leg das in ein überlazurt kechelin und güs luter essich dar uber eines fingers dik und las das ein tag und ein nacht stan und güs denn das obreste safft oben ab uff ein rib stein und tu dar under als ein haselnus gumi armoniacum und als ein erwis bol armenici und ein nuschal vol honges und rib das wol under

sprinkle in the powdered resin, stirring well until it begins to thicken so that a thread can be drawn out and then you will know it is ready.

If you want to make transparent parchment, take a piece of parchment of medium thickness and wash it several times in pure water, until no dirt comes out. Then press out the water thoroughly from the parchment with the palm of the hand. If you want to colour it green, take verdigris and grind it with strong vinegar and put it in a copper vessel and let it stand overnight and then strain it off into another copper vessel and do this three or four times. Then take the parchment and lay it in the liquid for a little while and then stretch it out on a frame and paint it over with varnish and then it will be ready.

If you wish to prepare verdigris, take some of this pigment and grind it with strong vinegar, added until it is a deep enough tint.

Here follows an article on how to make paper[80] better than it is generally made; also a description of how one can polish all kinds of stone; how stone can be softened so that it can be cut like cheese; how one can make a substance like agate which works in all ways like true agate; how to counterfeit agate in another way and how one can make a beautiful (artificial) ivory which can take a polish and is white and even more lovely than real ivory.

If you want to make varnish with which you can varnish anything so that it is beautiful, brilliant and lasting, take two or more egg whites—or as many as you require—and beat the white well, throwing away the scum. After this take $\frac{1}{2}$ oz. of gum arabic and $\frac{3}{4}$ oz. of either the gum of the almond tree or that of the cherry tree. The former is stronger, the latter clearer. The two gums should be ground together and you must put them in the above-mentioned white of egg and leave overnight to soften. Then grind it well together and add a paint-pot of honey. This must be all well mixed together by stirring and be kept in a glass receptacle well covered till required. Whatever colour is covered with this varnish becomes lovely and shiny and is also permanent. This varnish should be of the consistency of newly-run honey and dries quickly.

Again if you want to use this as a medium for tempering colours, put half an egg shell full of vinegar in it and if it is too thick, add some pure water and put it in a glass, first straining it through a cloth.

If you want to make a gold-size[81] that will never be moved by damp and which is good on iron or steel or tin or lead and indeed on any substance, take two parts ochre and a third part red lead and the fourth part Armenian bole and as much as you require of burnt white bone and a hazel nut of zinc vitriol. This colour must be

enander und in der diki als ein zerlossen honig und tp. das mit
itelm gumi wasser und müsch dar under vier troph. speichel also ist
si bereit.

Wiltu aber ein ander goldvarwe machen domit man mag silber
zin bli vergülden wo man si dar über strichest so schinet si als schön
vin gold dise varwe mache alsus zu dem esten nim aber virnis glas
oder mastix als vil und stos das zu bulver und ruters durch ein sib
und ein phunt ölis und las das öli vorhin erwallen und schum es
und rur das virnis bulver langsam in das heiss öli und rur es under
enander untz das virnis glas wol zergangen si und las es denn wol
senftekliche siden ane grosse hitze und rur es je bi der wile das es
nüt anbrounne und wenne es gerottet dikelecht werden so nim 4 lot
pic. goetum oder als vil aleo atustrinum oder als vil aleo tabellinum
weders du do nimst 4 lot zu 4 phunt virnis das verwet den virnis das
es schön gold varw wirt und disse driger eins soltu nemen und solt es
zu kleinen stupelin zerslagen und leg das in den virnis und rur es
wol under enander untz das die varwe wol under dem virnis zergangen
si und dar nach so versuch die gold varwe ze glicherwis als den virnis
und sich ob es einen vaden lot uff ziechen so ist sie wol gesotten und
ist ouch gut und gerecht an allen dingen und disse varwe gilt 1 lot
3 und dise varwe sol man rein behalten als den virnis und was man
mit diser varwe überstrichet es si silber zin oder bli das wirt schön
vin gold var das sol man an der sunne lan wol trotken werden so ist es
schön clor und ouch glantz und mag im kein wasser nüt geschaden.

Es folgt hier[83] nun wie man sol silber und gold uff legen trocken
und nas den aller besten sin uff berment uff pappir uff alter tafelen
etc.; wie man gold ufflegen sol an allen grund wie man ein gut assis
machen sol zu golde und zu silber das niemer geschrindet noch
gebrichet wie man sol uff bermet schön erhaben gold machen uff was
materien man gold und silber legen mag.

Aber ein schön rotelecht varwe die vil not ist geschaffen als
persilien varw man findet ein krut[84] an vil stetten in etlichen garten
und das selbe krut het vil rotte bletter und sint in ouch die stengel
rot und heisset blut krut und der des selbes krutes etwie vil gewinnet
und so es wol zitig ist das ist so es all ze mal itel rot ist die bletter und
ouch die stengel und so ist es an dem besten und het vil schöner roter
varwe und die bletter sol man alle ab dem stengel brechen und sol si
wol stossen und sol das rot saff uff ouch dur ein tuch gar us ringen
und ouch gebulverten alun dar in reren und reine wissi tuchlin in die
varwe trukent zwürent nach enander und tu in in aller der wis als dem
violvar und das ist ouch schön und vin.

Es Folgt wie man[85] brun rotte varwe machen um mit ze verwen uff

66

ground together with linseed oil and five drops of varnish and must be well strained through a cloth. And when you have laid it leave it to dry until it is only the least bit damp, and this mordant should be of the consistency of honey and it is the best gold-size that can be had.

For another gold-size, take *aleo*[82] *hepaticum* and *aleo titoclonium* —the same quantity of each, as much as you want—and put them in a glazed vessel and pour over them pure vinegar, till covered to the extent of a finger's breadth and leave to stand for twenty-four hours. Then pour the liquid off the top on to the grinding slab and mix with it as much as a hazel-nut of gum *armoniacum* and as much as a pea of Armenian bole and a small pot of honey and grind all well together. Again this should be of the consistency of liquid honey. Temper this with the usual gum water and mix with it four drops of spittle and then it is ready for use.

Again if you want to make another golden colour for painting over silver, tin or lead so that it looks like gold, make it as follows: To begin with, again take either *glassa* varnish or mastic and crush it to powder and pass it through a sieve into 1 lb. of oil but first let this oil cook and skim it, then slowly sprinkle the varnish into the hot oil and stir it together until the varnish is dissolved and let it then gently simmer without great heat, stirring it all the time so that it does not burn and when it begins to thicken take 2 ozs. of Greek pitch or the same quantity of *aleo atustrinum,* or of *aleo tabellinum* (whichever you use, take 2 ozs. to 4 lbs. varnish). This will turn the varnish into a lovely golden colour and whichever of these three you are using, must be crushed up small before being put into the varnish. Stir the ingredients well together so that the colouring matter is thoroughly dissolved in the varnish. After this, test the gold-size in the same way as you do for other varnishes to see whether it draws a thread, which means it is well cooked and right for use on anything. This colour is worth 3 shillings[?] per ½ oz. It must be kept clean like other varnishes and on whatever substance one puts this lacquer, whether silver, tin or lead, it will look a good bright golden colour. It must be allowed to dry throroughly in the sun in order that it may become beautifully clear and glossy. This varnish cannot be spoilt by water.

Here follows[83] a description of the best way to lay silver and gold both in the wet and the dry method, whether on parchment, on paper or on seasoned wooden panels; how to lay gold on any ground; how one can make a good foundation for gold and silver which will never shrink or split; and the whole art of raised gilding on parchment

leder und uff linin etc.; wie man schön violvarw verwen kann garn und linis und ouch uff leder; wie man schön vin grün bekömmt um zu verwen; wie man sol horn weich machen das man darus würket was man will und mans ouch giesset in ein jeglich form und es wider hert wirdet als vor.

Hiermit endet das Manuskript plötzlich. Wir haben also eine unvollständige Arbeit vor uns, da gewisse Rezepte fehlen und andere unfertig gelassen worden sind, während einige scheinbar aus ihrer unsprünglichen Position im Text an andere Stellen verpflanzt wurden. Doch sind dies nur kleine Unvollkommenheiten in einem Dokument, das sovieles von Bedeutung für Maler und Kunstgeschichtler enthält, und sie beeinträchtigen den Wert des Werkes als ein Ganzes nur wenig.

Beim Studium des Manuskriptes stellt es sich heraus, dass, obwohl ein grosser Teil des Textes der Kunst des Illuminierens gewidmet ist, sich das Werk keineswegs nur auf dieses Spezialgebiet beschränkt, sondern dass es sich auch weitgehend mit anderen Malarten beschäftigt. Der Leser wird bemerken, dass das Manuskript auf gewisse wichtige Punkte, die die Maltechnik früher Zeiten betrifft, Licht wirft, auf Themen, die bisher fast garnicht von Autoren auf diesem Gebiet behandelt worden sind. So scheint der besondere Wert dieser Arbeit in der Untersuchung dieser Entdeckungen zu liegen.

Eine ohne Zweifel jetzt festgestellte Tatsache, die bisher nur eine Vermutung gewesen ist, ist die, dass im Mittelalter in Nordeuropa Pergament-Leimfarben als selbständige Malmethode allgemein im Gebrauch waren, und dass sie nicht nur als Bestandteil der Gipsgrundierung verwendet wurden, über der Gemälde ausgeführt wurden. Es ist zudem einwandfrei klar, dass, obgleich Leimfarbe niemals zum Illuminieren verwendet wurde, diese Malart allgemein zum Ausmalen von Wandoberflächen, hölzernen Flächen, Leinwand usw. angewendet wurde. Es werden Beschreibungen für die Zubereitung von Leimfarben gegeben, denen Anweisungen für ihre Verdünnung zum Zweck des eigentlichen Malens folgen. Es geht auch aus diesen Anweisungen klar hervor, dass diese Farben mit Ölfirnis überstrichen werden mussten, um ihnen Leuchtkraft, und vor allem Dauerhaftigkeit zu verleihen.

Die Anweisungen für Beize-Vergoldungen sind auch von grosser Bedeutung, und der sich hierauf beziehende Abschnitt enthält ein wertvolles-Rezept für eine Goldmischung, die scheinbar in keiner anderen Abhandlung aus dieser Periode gefunden worden ist.

and a list of the materials on which gold and silver can be laid.

There is also a good red colour that is just as useful as brazil wood red. Sometimes in certain gardens a plant[84] is to be found growing which has a lot of red petals and even the stems are red. This is called bloodwort. Try if possible to pick a lot of these flowers, when they are in full bloom, for it is then that the petals and stems are all red together, the plant being then at its best and having a great deal of red colouring matter in it. You must break off both petals and stalks. Crush them well and wring the red juice from them through a straining cloth. Wring it out well, stirring into it powdered alum. Then, steep pieces of clean white rag in the colour and do this twice and treat it in every way as the violet rag colour, and it is a very lovely bright colour.

Here follows how one[85] can make a dark red colour with which to dye leather, linen etc. how to dye linen and wool violet colour and how to produce a beautiful green for dyeing; how one can soften horn and make it into any shape required by running it into a mould and letting it harden again.

Thus abruptly the manuscript comes to an end. The work as it stands will be seen to be incomplete owing to the fact that certain receipts are missing, others left unfinished, while some appear to have been moved from the position they originally occupied in the text. These however are small defects in a record containing so much that is of importance to both painter and art historian, and do little to detract from the value of the work as a whole.

A study of the manuscript reveals that although a great part of the text is devoted to the art of the illuminator it is by no means confined to this special field, but is also extensively concerned with other branches of art. The reader will observe that the manuscript brings to light certain important points regarding the techniques of painting in early times—points which till now have passed almost without comment from writers on the subject, and it is more especially in connection with these discoveries that the value of the work may be said to lie.

One fact established beyond doubt, which up to the present time had been a matter of surmise only, is that in medieval times, parchment size was in general use in Northern Europe as a painting medium in its own right and not merely as an ingredient of the gesso grounds on which paintings were executed. It is also clear that although seemingly never used in illumination, size painting was

In dem Abschnitt über Ölmalerei finden wir zudem die interessante Anspielung auf den Brauch, jeder Ölfarbe einige Tropfen Firnis während des Zerreibens hinzuzufügen. Zusätzlich wird sogar genau die Art des Firnis angegeben; und dies allein schon erhärtet die Theorie, dass die Sitte, einen aus Öl und Harz bestehenden Firnis zu benutzen, — wie bereits in den Aufzeichnungen des Theophilus erwähnt wird —, sich bis in spätere Zeiten erhalten hat.

Abschliessend ist zu sagen, dass Gelehrte, die an vergleichender Forschung auf dem Gebiet alter Malmethoden interessiert sind, das vorliegende Manuskript gern als wertvolle Ergänzung zu Cennini's *Libro dell'Arte* betrachten werden, indem es, wenngleich es weniger umfassend ist, die Theorien über die in Südeuropa verwendeten Malmethoden bestätigt. Wenn also das deutsche Handbuch zugegebener Maassen ein weniger ausgedehntes Gebiet umfasst als sein grosses italienisches Gegenstück, so dient es doch zweifellos dazu, die wenigen Lücken in Cennini's Lehren zu füllen, — Lücken, die ohne die zusätzlichen Kenntnisse, die das Strassburger Manuskript vermittelt, hätten ungefüllt bleiben müssen.

popular for decorating such surfaces as walls, wooden panels, canvas, etc. A clear description is given of making the size itself and instructions follow for its dilution as a painting vehicle. At the same time it is evident that these size colours required a final coat of oil varnish to give them brilliance and above all permanence.

Again the directions for mordant gilding are of great importance and the section dealing with this subject includes a valuable receipt for a certain gold-size, not apparently to be found in other treatises of the time.

Then also, in the section on oil-painting we find an interesting allusion to the practice of incorporating a few drops of varnish into each oil colour, during the process of grinding. Furthermore, the exact nature of the varnish used is given and this in itself endorses the theory that the custom of using a varnish composed of oil and resin, as given in the *Schedula* of Theophilus, must have continued into later times.

In conclusion, those interested in comparative research into early painting methods will readily appreciate the fact that the present manuscript although written on less comprehensive lines than Cennini's *Libro dell'arte* nevertheless forms a valuable adjunct to that work in supplying corroboration of the painting methods as used in South Europe. If therefore the German handbook is admittedly less extensive in scope than its great Italian counterpart it undoubtedly serves to fill those few gaps which occur in Cennini's teaching—gaps which must have remained unfilled but for the supplementary information supplied by the Strasburg manuscript.

APPENDIX
ANHANG

ANHANG

Wie schon in der Einleitung erwähnt wurde, behandelt diese Gruppe von Rezepten in keiner Weise die Kunst der Malerei. Sie ist daher aus dem eigentlichen Manuskript herausgenommen und hier an das Ende des Buches gestellt worden. Die Übersetzer sind der Ansicht, dass, hätte man diese Sammlung von allen möglichen "Haushaltswinken" an ihrer ursprünglichen Stelle belassen, dies nur dazu dienen würde, die Aufmerksamkeit des Lesers von dem Hauptgegenstand dieses Dokumentes abzulenken. Die im folgenden Abschnitt beschriebenen Verfahren erstrecken sich von detaillierten Beschreibungen der Seifenbereitung bis zu phantastischen umständlichen kosmetischen Rezepten, von denen man offenbar im Mittelalter Gebrauch machte. Diese Anweisungen sind, im Gegensatz zu denen über Malerei, für den Leser oft langweilig und kaum der Mühe wert. Sie sind ausserdem zu veraltet und bruchstückhaft, um nutzbringende Erläuterungen zu sein; aus diesem Grunde ist kein Versuch gemacht worden, sie mit Anmerkungen zu versehen.

Vielleicht möchte sich ein Wissenschaftler, den die Verfahren mittelalterlicher Chemie interessieren, eines Tages bereitfinden, die Brauchbarkeit dieser seltsamen und überalterten Rezepte zu prüfen und auf diese Weise mehr Licht auf den in diesem Teil des Manuskriptes behandelten Gegenstand zu werfen.

WILTU ABER DUT TINTEN MACHEN von substancie. Accipe unam partem de calce fino et duas partes cinerej clarifatas et fac lixivium et distalla perfiltrum. Nim ein rousches ei und leg es uff die lengi swimmet es denne oben an so ist si stark genug und nim die lougen und tu si in einen reinen kessel und ein für darunder und tu denn das unschlit darin und las es sieden als lang untz es sich lat uff zichen als ein lin wenn du das sichest. So tu der langen mer darin so wirt es je lenger je diker nim schön wis saltz und wirf es langsan dar in als lang bis das du sichest das es dünne werde so nim den ein rur holz und grif den domit in den kessel und nim sin dar an har us und hab es uff und blibet di materie obenan an den holtz und rünnet das wasser abe so het es saltz genug dar nach sol es in den Wasser sieden als lang bis das du es nimest uff deinen finger und trukest es sichest du das es also hert ist das es nut vil me wassers hat so hat es sin genug dar noch so nim daz für davon und las es sich enwenig setzen und wenn es sich enwenig gesetzet so nim es uff das rur holtz gewelt es dir an der wisi so güs es, ist es aber nüt wiss genug so las es stan übernacht und las es külen und snid es den us dem kessel und wenne du es

74

APPENDIX

As mentioned in the Introduction, this group of receipts, in no way concerned with the practice of painting, has been removed from the body of the Manuscript and placed here at the end of the book. The translators believe that had this collection of sundry 'household hints' been left in its original position, it could only have served to distract the reader's attention from the main subject matter of the document. The processes described in the section below range from detailed descriptions of soap-making to those of fantastically elaborate cosmetic preparations evidently in use in medieval times ! These instructions—unlike those concerned with painting—often make tedious and unrewarding reading. They are also of too archaic and fragmentary a nature to permit of useful comment and, for this reason, no attempt has been made at annotation.

Perhaps at some future date a practical scientist interested in the processes of medieval chemistry will be prepared to test the viability of these curious and obsolete receipts and thus help to throw further light on the subject matter of this part of the manuscript.

AGAIN IF YOU WISH to make good ink out of *substancie*.

Accipe unam partem de calce fino et duas partes cinereje clarifactis et fac lixivium et distilla per filtrum. (Take one part of purified lime and two parts of sieved ashes and make a lye and strain it through a cloth). Take a raw egg and put it in the lye. If it floats on the surface, it means that the lye is strong enough. Pour this into a clean pan and put it on the fire, then put in the tallow and let it boil until you can draw up a thread when you test it. Next add more lye and the longer you boil it the thicker it will be. After this take good white salt and throw it in gradually until you see that it is getting thin. Then take a stirring rod and plunge it in the pan and take it out again and if the solid part sticks to the wooden rod and the water has considerably reduced, the mixture has been sufficiently salted. After this the tallow must go on boiling in the water until on taking it up on your finger you find that it is hard when you press it and also that not much water remains in the pan. This means it has been cooked long enough. After this take the pan off the fire and let the mixture settle for a little while and when it has stood thus for a time, take it up on the stirring rod and if it is as white as you wish it to be, run it off [into moulds]. If however it is not white enough, let it stand overnight and when it is

hast us gesnitten so güs das Wasser us das dar under ist und renig den
kessel wol dar nach in ungelöschen kalk und gemein eschen doch mer
kalkes den der eschen und güs dar uff ein warm wasser und mische es
durch enander untz das wasser die bitterkeit an sich züchet dar nach
las es luter werden und seig es aber — distilla per filtrum — und
güs es in den kessel und saltz es wol dar nach die usgeschnitten seiff
und snid si in den kessel in das selb wasser und las es sieden als lang
und nim es uff einen finger und truk ob es enwenig sitze als vor und
güs als vor so gewinstu seiffen wis und gut. Wiltu aber gut seiffen
machen nim zu dem ersten 2 lib. lebendigen kalk und ein lib weideschen und 1 lib wisses win steines und ½ lib aluns und 8 lot spangrünes und diesi stük stosse alle ze samen ze bulver und güs darüber
lougen die mit eschen gemacht si und der lougen sol sin 12 moss und
die lougen sol zu dem vierden mol uber das bulver gegossen werden
und wenne es zu dem vierden mol luter us gat so ist die louge
bereit. So nim 6 lib oder 8 kuchen unslitz oder scheffins oder widrin
und· zersnide den unslit ze kleinen stüken in einem zuber und güs
die vorḡñ loug in den zuber über die stükelin und teke den zuber wol
mit einem lid und lasse in also stan 14 tag ze beissen so zergat das
unslit in der lougen dar no so güs alles das in den zuber ist in ein
grossen kessel und henke in über ein für und lasse in senfteklichen
sieden das es vil nach dem halbteil in geseid und nim denn 1 fierling
oleis und rur das in den kessel und las es dar mit erwallen und hab
denn den kessel ab und las in übernacht stan untz das daz er wol
erkaltet und des morgentz sol man oben ab nemen was do gestanden
ist und hert ist das sol man under enander knetten mit einem löffel
das es wol gebert si und denn sol mans truken in ein überlazurt
kacheln die da vier eggecht si und nim den ein brett und ubersege
das mit gerittertem kalk und leg die kuchen dar uff und lasse si ligen
14 tag untz si an dem wind wol truken werdent so ist es bereit und
ist gut und wis.

Wiltu aber gut seiffen machen nim 2 lib unschlit, buchloug ein
halb mos, Kalk Wasser ein mas und seig dor in wisses hundes kat
und ein halb hant vol gebrantz saltz und ein wenig weider eschen und
lass es sieden das es wert recht als ein bri wiltu wissen wenn is
genug si so tu ein troph oder zwen uff einen stein also heiss geramet
es so ist es genug und tu ir du weist wol. Wiltu gut seiffen machen
nim 2 lib lebendig kalk 4 lib weidëschen und 1 lib trusen eschen und
süde die in hundert quart wassers untz an 25 quart denn leg ein
eij in dieselben lougen swimet es enber so ist si stark genug nim von
der lugen 10 lib und seiffen unslitz ouch 10 lib. und süde das als lang
das es dik werde und rure es stetenklich und güs sie in formen.

cool cut it out [of the pan]. This done, pour off the water that is underneath. Afterwards clean out your pan well with unslaked lime and coarse ashes, even more lime than ashes; pouring on warm water and stirring this well round so that the water washes away any traces of lime. Afterwards, let the liquid [which you set aside] become clear (by settling) and then strain it and pour it back into the cleaned pan and salt it. Next add the roughly cut up soap and cut it up small in this same water. Let it boil for as long as before, taking it up as previously on the finger and pressing it to test if it will stay. Then pour the soap out [into a mould] as before. In this way you will obtain a perfectly white soap.

If you wish to make good soap in another way take 2 lbs. quick lime and 1 lb. of willow wood ash and 1 lb. of white [probably calcined] tartarum and ½ lb. alum and 8 oz. verdigris (!) and pound all these together to powder and pour over them some lye made from wood ash. You should have 12 *mas* of lye and this should be poured over the powder four times and when you have done this for the fourth time, it becomes clear and ready for use. Then take 6 to 8 lbs. of cakes of tallow or *scheffins* or *widrin* [lard?] and cut them up into small pieces putting them into a large vat and pour over them the beforementioned lye. Then cover the vat tightly with a lid and let it stand for a fortnight to steep. In this way the tallow dissolves readily in the lye. Next pour off all that is in the vat into a large cauldron and hang it up over the fire and let it simmer slowly till the mixture is reduced by more than half. Then take a *fierling* of oil and stir it into the pot and let it boil up with the rest. Then take the pot off the fire and let it stand overnight till it is quite cold and the next day the part which has risen to the top and is solid, must be taken off and be pressed together with a spoon to make it into a lump. This must be pressed into a rectangular glazed vessel. Then take a board and strew it with sieved lime and lay the tablets [of soap] on this and let them stay there for a fortnight. They should be left in a draught in order to dry thoroughly. Prepared in this way [the soap] will be ready for use and be pure white.

Another way of making good soap is to take 2 lbs. tallow, ½ *mas* of washing lye, 1 gall. lime water and sieve into this, white *hundeskat* and ½ a handful of salt petre and a little willow ash and let it all boil together till the mixture becomes as thick as a pulp. When you wish to know whether it is sufficiently cooked, put a drop or two of it on a stone [The rest of this sentence is missing].

Wiltu wissen wie man horn güst als bli, so nim das die hörner ab filent von den horn ———— ———— und leg es in einen hafen und nim weideschen zwei teil und kalkes das dritteil und güs das über die materie gang und las den hafen siden un rur es mit einem isen löffel das es über dik werde als ein mus wiltu den rot haaen so nim minie und tu die darunder die klein si und rur es denn untz das es rot werde und güs denn die materie in ein form und las es truken und nim denn bilsen wurtz und zertrieb die klein und tu die denn uff das horn so truknet es schier und wirt es ganz form und beschab es mit einer guter schaben so wirt es luter und machest do von was du wilt das wirt schön und gut.

Wiltu aber horn giessen so nim horn und snetze das klein tu es in ein long di zu seiffen gut si und süd es darin untz das es zergang und die loug davon gesüd und güs es denn in was form du wilt also wirt es und belibet ouch also wiltu es verwen so machtu geriben varw dar under tun die wil es lind ist in denne hafen was varwe du darin tust also wirt ouch das horn es hilfet wisses horn zu verwen und nüt swartzes du macht schiltgiessen oder blashörner oder was du wilt haben.

Wiltu aber horn giessen und weich machen das man drus druket was man wil und mans ouch güsset in ein jeglich form und es wider hert wirt ze dem ersten sol man nemen hornes als vil man wil und das horn sol vorhin 4 wuchen alt sin und wol bedeket sin und nement 1 lib kalkes der nüt nas si und halb als vil weideschen oder win trusen eschen und 8 lot winsteines und ouch als vil saltzes und wischent das alles zusäme unter die horn und land das alles mit enander wol erwallen in einem kessel und giessend denn dar us ein luter loug zwarent noch en ander und behaltent das wasser wol bedeket in einem hafen untz das man sin bedarff und wenn man das horn weich machen so legent das horn in den hafen in das wasser und land es stan 8 tag in den Wasser so wirt das horn weich und ist us (hier ist e twas ausgestrichen.) Ist er schuldig so wirt der spiegel zehant bleich nim einen nüwen spiegel und leg in in ein wasser eines Brunnen und las in ligen über nacht in einer nüwen schüssel und dis morgents schrib die Wort dar uff mit Rappenblut geschriben und leg den spiegel uff einen tisch oder war du wilt und wer dar.

Wiltu machen ein wasser und wenns man es in ein Ampel tut und ein spiegel. Nim wasen die milch hant so vil du wilt und schup si rein und weide si und tu si denn in einen überlazurten hafen und spreng aroma darüber und teke den hafen oben gar wol zu mit becht und setz in denn in einer fulen mist und las darin stan 8 wuchen so nim in denn harus so sint die visch ze wasser worden so

If you wish to make good soap, take 1 lb. quicklime, 4 lbs. wood ashes, 1 lb. brickdust and boil them in 100 qts. water till this is reduced to 25 qts. Then put an egg in this lye. If it floats to the surface [the lye] is strong enough.

Take 10 lbs. lye, 10 lbs. soap tallow and boil this till it becomes thick. Then stir it round well and run it off into moulds.

If you wish to learn how to liquefy horn as if it were lead, procure horns at the time of year at which they are shed from the animal and put them in a pot. Then take wood ashes 2 parts, lime 1 part [with water] and pour this all over the [pieces of] horn. Let it boil in the pot and stir it with an iron spoon till it turns to a pulp. Should you wish to make it red, take some red lead [powder] and add it to the horn, stirring the whole together till it becomes red. Then run off the melted horn into a mould and let it set. Then take hen-bane root and grind it up fine and powder it over the horn to speed up drying and help it to keep its shape. If you scrape it with a good scraper it will take a polish, and you can make whatever you like out of it; it will be sound and will keep well.

If you wish to liquefy horn in another way, take some and shave it up small and put it in the kind of lye used for soap making. Stir it into this until it dissolves and then boil it up in the lye. Next pour [the horn] into any mould you wish and it will take the shape and later will not warp. Then, if you wish to tint it, add powdered pigment to it while it is [still] soft in the pan. The horn will take the colour of whatever pigment you put in. For colouring it is advisable to use white horn rather than black. You can mould coats of arms and fashion trumpets or whatever else you like [with horn treated in this way].

Again, if you wish to melt or soften horn so that it can be moulded into any desired form and then harden again, first take as much horn as you require and this must be at least four weeks old and it must be well kept covered. Then take 1 lb. of quick lime and half as much willow ash or vine twig ash and 8 ozs. of tartar and the same quantity of salt and this must all be mixed together with the horn and then all be boiled up together in a cauldron; then pour off clear lye [by straining] twice in succession . . . and keep the liquid well covered in a bowl until it is needed and when one wishes to soften the horn lay it in the liquid in the bowl. Let it steep for eight days by which time the horn will have become soft. [Here something is struck out]. If it is faulty, the mirror will at once turn whitish. So take another mirror and put it in clean well water and leave it overnight in a glazed dish. In the morning, write the word on it in the blood of a black

tu das wasser in ein ampel und tek ein spiegel dar uber so schinet das wasser als ein recht licht. Wiltu machen fin gut lazur als mans übermer macht so lasse dir machen ein silbrin büchse und nim denn "calcem mortuum" der wol gebrannt si und rib in gar klein und tu das in win essig der gut si und der essich sol zwürent wol gesaltzen sin un versuch es uff der Zunge dar noch güs den essich uff den kalk und mache es als dik als ein müs und nim das selb und tu es in die büchse und vermach die büchse wol mit an der stat do die büchse ze samen gat und setz sie in einen mist und las si dar in stan 4 Wuchen do noch nim si har us und tu die varwe in ein bekin und las sie truken an der sunne.

Wiltu machen gut lazur nim den allerbesten win als vil du wilt und leg dar in enwenig alunes das der alun dar in zergange und tu denn den selben win uff ungelöschen kalk und mache dar us ein louge und güs die louge in ein drinaltig sekelin und ouch en wenig esche dar inne si und lasse das louffen in ein bekin das tu als lang untz es beginne blawen so nim denn geschaben persilie und den alun der do geweschen ist die du in den win hest geleit und leg es denn in ein louge und las es darin ligen über nacht und nim es denn des morgentz wider her us und henk es aber über das bekin und tu das als lang untz das du dich dunke das es fin genug habe so rur es und trenke es mit lougen zwürent oder dri stunt so wirt es gut lazur.

Wer sin hand oder sin füsse oder sin hut welle wiss machen der neme blauen gilian würtz und derre die wol und stosse si ze kleinen bulver und nim bonen mel und mandel kernen meil und nim seiffen und leg si in warmen essich dar mit win gemischet si und nim ein gantz ei und kloph das alles ze samen und wesche dich do mit und solt das tun 8 tag wer aber welle schön wiss hend allen lib haben der sol nemen wasser wurtzen und sol die klein zerschniden recht wurplecht und sol die saft sieden in oule und wesche do mit din antlit oder din hende. Wiltu das nit tun so bestrich dich mit pharren mist oder mit eselmilch und in des Abends lubstikel würtzelz vil vast in wasser und wesche des morgendes din Anlit mit oder trink ze meigen tuben croaph safft in honig gesotten das machet dir gar wunder schön hut. Oder nim smer und speke und zerlasse die zwei under enander und tu es in kalt gossen lougen und las da innen ligen 3 tag und in essich 3 tag und in milch 3 tag und den tragent und der mastik lege in win und las das über nacht ligen uff den totten stein und den syat soltu brennen in einem ziegel und die garnfran soltu zertriben und zerstossen und tu dis alles zu enander es wirt ein vil kospar salb und do mit soltu slaben die Antlit und die hend so werdent si dir als milch und als blut.

horse and lay the mirror on a table or wherever you wish and whoever . . .

If you want to make a liquid to keep in an ampulla covered with a glass take small fish in the right condition, as many as you need, clean them well, slit them up and put them in a glazed dish, sprinkling *Aroma* over them and cover the dish with a piece of bladder. Place in a manure heap and let it stay there eight weeks. The fish will then be reduced to a liquid, which pour into an ampulla covering it with a piece of glass. The liquid will shine brilliantly like a light. If you wish to make an especially good blue, as it is made overseas, have a silver box made and then take slaked lime that has been well calcined and grind it very thoroughly with wine vinegar of good quality. The vinegar should be thoroughly salted. Having tested it with the tongue, pour it on the lime making this into a paste. Then take it up and put it in the box. Then seal the lid well all round the aperture and place it in a manure heap and let it remain there for four weeks. After this, take it out and put the colour in a basin and let it dry in the sun.

If you wish to make good blue, take as much as you need of best quality wine and put in it a little alum, letting it dissolve. Then put some of this same wine on some quick lime and make a lye from it. Then pour this lye into a small bag of threefold thickness into which some ash has been put and let it drip into a basin. Do this until the liquid begins to look blue. Next take some brazil wood shavings and the alum which you soaked in the wine. Then lay these in lye and leave to stand overnight and in the morning take it out again and hang it over a basin. Leave it until you think that it has dripped long enough. Continue stirring and adding more lye two or three times and it will be a good blue.

Whoever wishes to whiten their hands, feet or skin should take lily bulbs and dry them well; then crush them to a fine powder with bean flour and ground almonds. Then take soap and let this all soak in warm vinegar mixed with wine and take a whole egg and beat it all up together and anoint yourself with this for eight days running. Whoever wishes to have lovely white hands that are admired by all, should take *wasser wurtsel* and cut them up small with great diligence and then must boil them in oil and bathe the face and hands with [the resulting ointment].

If you do not wish to do this, anoint yourself with bracken manure or with donkey's milk and at evening time with the roots of *Liebstökcel* (*levisticum officinale*) soaked in water and in the morning wash your face with it, or in May drink the juice of *Taubenkropf* (*Fumaria*

Wiltu machen ein salb wenn du einen schwartzen pherit den ruggen mit salbest so wirt er im wis ein newerfender der in dem meigen gewangen ist und zershnid den in regem wasser und süd in in dem regen wasser und nim das schmalz oben ab und nim denn wisser wiroch und las den zergan in einer phanne und tp. das underenander und tu es denne in ein büchse und wass schwartzer rosen du best-richet diewerdent wis.

Wiltu ein gut stimm gewinnen so nim laque riciem 1 mes und ganfras 2 mes und tragens zwei mes und tp. das mit wasser und heb es lang under deiner Zungen oder süd einer nüwen kes und knobloch in milch und is das und trinke die milch so gewinnet du gut stimme. Wiltu das nüt tun so nim aber nisussen die wachsen in miesch uff alten eichen und nim ouch kriesch bouw in den appenteg *lacquericiem* und ein wurtz heisst *crisliana* und nim ouch gleigen wurtz und isofen crut und enis und venkel wurtzel venkelsamen und zimmet und honig und zucker und süd die alle sammet mit enander in wasser in einen nüwen hafen und tu ouch masticem zu den dingen und so si si wol geschument werdent und dar nach vil wol gesüdet so nim si von dem füre und teke den hafen wol mit einem schönen tuch und dar uff einen nüwen tekel und du wilt schlaffen gan so nim des wassers einen guten trunk und so du des morgendes uff stast so tu ouch also so wirt dir ein gut stimme. Gelaob mirs wand ich versucht es nie. Wiltu das ouch nüt tun so nim umb sand 10 mes do vor oder do nach holder loub wen es wol gewachsen sin und doch nüwe si und derre es an der sunnen vil wol das es sich lasse zertriben und bütel es auch vil klein und nim vil wis ingher und stosse das ouch vil kleine und es selben den siebenden teil zu den bulver der holder blattern und tu denn zu den zwein bulvern und halb als vil zuckers so der zweger bulver si und isse denn des bulvers an dem morgent früg ein halb eiger schal vol. Wiltu das nüt tun so nim senf und stosse den in einen mürsel und ribe das vil klein und tp. das mit honig seme und mach dar us vil klene kügelli und is di vastendex.

Wiltu schön lang har machen nim lylien und brunne die und us der eschen mach ein lougen und twach da mit din houpt dike. Wiltu das din har nüt grawe so brenne Költörse ze eschen und do mit mach ein loug und twach din har dik mit. oder nim Betenien bletter und wisse weiden bletter und süde die in geissiner milch und wenn sie wol gesüdet so tu es in ein stark lini tuch und truk es wol us und strich din houpt vil fast do mit.

Wiltu din har nüt graue so nim eines alten hundes milch und salb din har da mit wol fast ze grund — Wem das har us riset der nem linsamen und brune den uff einem ziegel und setze dar under ein

officinalis) boiled with honey, this gives you a marvellously beautiful skin.

Or take butter and lard and melt the two together and put the mixture into cold lye and leave it for three days, then for 3 days in vinegar and then for three days in milk. Next put tragacanth and mastic in wine and let them steep overnight in a stone vessel and you must heat the mixture in an earthenware dish, and you must crush and grind *Geum urbanum* and all these you must mix together. This is a most expensive ointment but if you anoint your face and hands with it they will be pink and white like milk and roses.

If you wish to make an ointment, which if you anoint a black mole [blemish or wart] with it the same turns white, take a *newerfender* that can be caught in May and slice it into rain water and boil it in the same and skim the fat off and take white incense and let it dissolve in a pan and mix all together and then put it in a box and whatever black blemish you anoint with it will become white.

If you wish to improve you voice take *lacquericiem* [liquorice] and *geum urbanum* 2 measures and tragacanth 2 measures and mix it with water and keep it for some time under the tongue or cook some fresh cheese and garlic in milk and eat it, the former, and drink the latter, and your voice will be improved. If you do not want to do this, you can take *nisussem* which grows in moss on old oak-trees and the leaves of the cherry tree, and from the chemist *lacquericiem* [liquorice] and a root called *crisliana* (*Helleborus niger*) and take also the bulbs of *Iris Germanica* and *Hyssopus officinalis* root and aniseed and fennel root and fennel seeds and cinnamon and honey and sugar and boil them all together in water in an earthenware pot and add some mastic to the rest and when the mixture has been well skimmed and after that allowed to cook thoroughly, take the pan off the fire and cover it carefully with a nice cloth and place over this a clean lid. On going to bed, take a drink of this potion and on rising in the morning, do the same and your voice will be much improved. Believe me, although I have never tried [the remedy]. If, however, you do not want to do this either, take about 10 *mes* more or less of elder leaves when they are at their prime and are still fresh and dry them in the sun until they are in the right condition for grinding and powder them very small and take a large quantity of white ginger and pound it also very small and it should be in amount $\frac{1}{7}$ of the elder leaf powder and next add to these two powders half as much sugar when the two are well ground to powder and then take half an egg shell full of the powder early in the morning.

If you do not want to do this, then take mustard and pound it in a

schüssel und enpach das verbrunnen oul darin und salbe sin houpt
ze grund fast damit. Nim nuss kernen wie vil du wilt und stosse die
vast und tu si denn in ein tüchlin und hab es zu den für untz das es
wol warm werde und bestrich din houpt das dir von deinem houpt
schön har wachse als gespunnen gold so nim in dem *aber ellen*
[apenteken ?] espin bollen und derre die in einen lewen ofen der nüt
ze heiss si und nim si den und stoss si wol zu kleinem bulver und so du
das als morn dir houpt wilt zwachen so tu des selben stuppes zwo
eiger schalen vol als nacht in die lougen und las dar inne uber nacht
ligen. Twache den morndes din houpt mit.

Jetzt folgen einige artikel wie man solle machen gut fin halfenbein,
ein wasser der tugend und ein trank der tugend zwei wasser die luter
sind als ein brun — und wenn man sie under enander tut so werdent
si als gelegli milch. Wie man die fliegen alle wol bringen kann in
einen kreis die in dem huse sind.

mortar and grind it very fine and mix it with honey and of this make tiny balls and take them fasting.

If you want to have lovely long hair, take lilies and burn them and make a lye with the ashes, and wash your head thoroughly with this. If you wish your hair not to turn grey, burn *Koltorse* [*cabbage stalk*] to ashes and make a lye and thoroughly wash your hair with this or take betony[?] leaves and the leaves of white willows and boil them in goat's milk and when they are thoroughly cooked, strain through a strong linen cloth and saturate your head well with it.

If you do not want grey hair, take the milk of an old bitch and anoint your hair and scalp well with it. Whoever is losing their hair should take linseed and cook it on an earthenware dish and place a dish underneath to catch the overflow and anoint your scalp thoroughly with this. Take the kernels of nuts as many as you want and pound them thoroughly and place them in a cloth and put them over the fire [in a pan] and rub this into the scalp in order to make beautiful hair grow like spun gold. Procure from the apothecary *gemma populi* [the buds of the aspen tree] and dry them in an oven that is not too hot and take them out, grind them to a fine powder, and if you want to wash your head the following morning, put two egg shells full of this powder in lye the evening before and let it steep overnight. Then in the morning, rinse your head in it.

Now follows an article on how to make fine ivory, how a potion of great virtue is made, how by mixing two liquids which are themselves as clear as well-water the resulting liquid is as opaque as milk. Also how one can bring all the flies that are in the house together into a circle.

NOTES
ANMERKUNGEN

ANMERKUNGEN

1 *Truknet*

Diese Sitte, Farbstoffe auf einer Platte trocknen zu lassen, nach dem vorläufigen Zermahlen entweder in reinem Wasser oder mit einem Bindemittel, scheint in frühen Zeiten sehr üblich gewesen zu sein, wenn man Farben zum Illuminieren vorbereitete. Der Hauptzweck war wohl der, den genauen Farbton zu prüfen, nachdem das Mahlen, Mischen und Wieder-Trocknen ihn etwas verändert hatte.

2 *Nuschal*

Es ist nicht möglich gewesen, die genaue Bedeutung des Wortes *nuschal* festzustellen, obgleich es sich um eine Art von kleinem Topf handeln muss. Das alte mittel-hochdeutsche Wort *nuosch* bedeutet Trog oder Rille, und das moderne hochdeutsche *Schale* bedeutet Schale, kegelförmiges Gefäss, Vase, Tasse oder Untertasse. So mögen die beiden Worte in *nuschal* verbunden worden sein. Dieses Wort ist daher hier entweder mit Topf oder Maltopf übersetzt worden, entsprechend dem Zusammenhang, in dem es vorkommt. An manchen Stellen scheint das Gefäss, das benutzt wurde, nur ein winziges Töpfchen für eine kleine Menge Farbe zum Illuminieren gewesen zu sein, an anderen Stellen bezeichnet *nuschal* ein Gefäss, das gross genug war, um darin zermahlene Farbstoffe zu waschen und zu verrühren.

Ernst Berger in seinen *Beiträge zur Entwicklungsgeschichte der Maltechnik* zitiert das Wort als *muschal*, da er annahm, es bedeute *Muschel*. Bei Einsicht in das Manuskript erweist es sich aber als ein Fehler, das 'N' durch ein 'M' zu ersetzen. Tatsächlich wurden Muscheln aller Arten weitgehend von Künstlern früherer Zeiten als Malgefässe benutzt. Andererseits hätte man das Waschen und Verrühren von Farbstoffen niemals zufriedenstellend in so flachen und kleinen Gefässen wie Muschelschalen ausführen können.

3 *Gumi*

Mann kann annehmen, dass Gummi Arabicum der erwähnte Gummi war. Dieser wird aus Akazienbäumen gewonnen und wird jetzt noch in Krystallform in Drogerien verkauft. Er ist ein ausgezeichnetes Beimischmittel für Wasserfarben. In zahllosen Maler — Manuskripten werden Rezepte für seine Herstellung gegeben, siehe:

Illuminier Buch von Valentin Boltz.

The Whole Art of Limning von Nicholas Hilliard.

Original Treatises von Mrs. Merrifield.

De Arte Illuminandi, von einem anonymen Autor des 14. Jahrhunderts,
   übersetzt aus dem Lateinischen des Naples Codex von D. V. Thompson,

Das letzte, das allgemein unter dem Titel The Naples Codex bekannt ist, enthält eine besonders genaue und klare Beschreibung der Zubereitung von Gummi Arabicum.

4 *Horn*

Das deutsche Wort *Horn* scheint fast dieselbe Bedeutung zu haben wie *nuschal*, aber wahrscheinlich bezeichnet es ein engeres, tieferes Gefäss. Das alt-englische Wort Ink-horn deutet auf seine Form hin. Daher ist es mit Tintenfass übersetzt

NOTES

¹ *Dry, Truknet*
This practice of letting pigment dry on the slab after a preliminary grinding either in pure water or with a binding medium appears to have been quite usual in early times when paint was being prepared for illuminating. The chief use seems to have been to test the exact tone of the colour after the grinding, mixing and redrying had slightly altered its appearance.

² *Pot, Nuschal*
It has not been possible to establish the exact significance of the word *nuschal*, though it must mean a small pot of some kind. The Old Middle High German word *nuosch* meant a trough or groove and the modern German *schale* means bowl, cone shaped vessel, vase, cup or saucer, so the two may well have been combined to make *nuschal*. This word has therefore been here translated as either pot or paint-pot according to the context in which it is found. In places, the vessel to be used seems to be a tiny jar for holding the illuminators small quantity of paint, in others *nuschal* denotes a jar large enough for ground-up pigment to be washed and stirred round in.

Ernst Berger in his *Beiträge zur Entwicklungsgeschichte der Maltechnik* gives the word as *muschal* taking this to mean *muschel* mussel shell. Reference to the manuscript itself, however, proves the substitution of an 'm' for the 'n' to be erroneous. It is true that shells of all sorts were widely used by artists in early times as paint-pots, on the other hand, however, the washing and stirring of pigment could never have been successfully carried out in a vessel as shallow nor indeed as small as a mussel shell.

³ *Gum Arabic. Gumi*
It can be assumed that gum arabic was the gum referred to. This is the gum of the acacia tree which is still sold at chemists in crystal form and makes an excellent water colour medium: In countless painters' manuscripts receipts are given for its preparation, see:

Illuminier Buch by Valentin Boltz.
The Whole Art of Limning by Nicholas Hilliard.
Original Treatises by Mrs. Merrifield.
De Arte Illuminandi by an anonymous 14th Century author, translated from the Latin of the Naples Codex by D. V. Thompson.

This last, generally known as The Naples Codex, contains an especially concise and clear description of the preparation of gum arabic.

⁴ *Ink-Pot. Horn*
The German word *horn* would seem to be almost synonymous with *nuschal* though it probably denotes a somewhat narrower deeper vessel. The Old English word Ink-horn suggests the shape. Accordingly it has been translated as ink-pot except

worden, mit Ausnahme von den Fällen, in denen es sich augenscheinlich um ein grösseres Gefäss handelt, wo das Wort Topf benutzt wurde.

5 Zinober

Cinnabar war der ursprüngliche alte Name für die Farbe, die wir jetzt Zinnober nennen. Dieses rote Quecksilber-Sulphit war in klassischen Zeiten in seinem natürlichen Zustand wohlbekannt. Wie Plinius berichtet, kam es fast ausschliesslich aus Spanien. Er erwähnt es ausserdem als eine der kostbarsten Farben auf des Maler's Palette. Im Mittelalter wurde ein grosser Teil des verwendeten Zinnobers künstlich hergestellt, und man nimmt an, dass gegen Ende des 12. Jahrhunderts das fabrizierte Mineral allgemein im Gebrauch war; es ist aber nicht bekannt, wann genau das Geheimnis seiner Herstellung entdeckt wurde, siehe *Materials of Medieval Painting*, D. V. Thompson.

Cinnabar sollte nicht mit cinabrese, einer natürlichen roten sinopia, die mit geweisstem Kalk zusammen gemahlen wurde, verwechselt werden. Diese Farbe wurde von der Toskanischen Schule sehr häufig in der Freskomalerei verwendet. Beispiele von ihrer Anwendung kann man jetzt im Campo Santo in Pisa studieren. Dort wurde im Jahre 1945 durch Kriegsschaden die Oberfläche der grossen Fresken zerstört und dadurch wurde die darunter befindliche Lage der ursprünglichen Untermalung, die sogenannte *Sinopie*, blossgelegt.

6 Eyger Clor

Das Wort *eyger clor* bedeutet einfach Eiweiss, aber dort, wo der deutsche Ausdruck benutzt wurde, um den aus Eiweiss hergestellten Malstoff zu bezeichnen, wurde es im Englischen mit Glaire übersetzt. Glaire zum Malen wird in folgender Weise zubereitet: Man tue ein Eiweiss in eine Schüssel und schlage es mit einem Schneebesen so lange bis der Schaum so steif ist, dass man die Schüssel umstülpen kann, ohne dass sich der Schaum bewegt. Danach giesse man über das geschlagene Eiweiss ein dreiviertel Glas Wasser und lasse die Mischung über Nacht stehen; dann wird der Schaum entfernt und die Flüssigkeit ist gebrauchsfertig. In diesem Manuskript befindet sich auf Seite 29 noch ein anderes Rezept zur Glaire-Herstellung, das vielleicht weniger Zeit als das hier angeführte beanspruchte: es scheint aber weder solch guter noch solch sauberer Vorgang zu sein. Glaire für Benutzung als Firnis wurde ohne Hinzufügung von Wasser geschlagen. Siehe Cennini's *Trattato*.

7 Lougen

Eine Lösung von Pottasche, die durch Kochen feingesiebter Holzasche oder Asche von allerlei Sorten Pflanzen, unter Hinzufügung einer kleinen Menge von ungebranntem Kalk, hergestellt wurde. In diesem Falle mag es eine Lauge gewesen sein, die nur mit Holzasche und Wasser zubereitet wurde.

8 Saffrans

Die Blütenblätter und Narben dieser Blumen, nachdem sie getrocknet und zu Pulver zerrieben worden waren, wurden vielfach als Färbemittel benutzt, aber auch als Farbe von Illuminatoren hochgeschätzt. Die Farbe wurde manchmal allein durch Wasser herausgezogen, in manchen Fällen wurden aber auch Essig oder Harzlösungen verwendet.

in those cases where a larger container is evidently intended, when it is rendered as jar.

5 *Vermilion. Zinober*

Cinnabar was the ancient name for the colour we now call vermilion. This red sulphide of mercury in its natural state was well known in classic times, coming almost entirely from Spain, as Pliny records. He mentions it also as being one of the most precious colours of the painters palette. In medieval times much of the vermilion used was made artificially, and by the end of the 12th Century the manufactured mineral is believed to have been in general use, although it is not known at what precise date the secret of its manufacture was discovered, see *Materials of Medieval Painting*, D. V. Thompson.

Cinnabar should not be confused with cinabrese, a natural red sinopia ground together with lime white and much used by the Tuscan school for fresco painting. Examples of the use of this colour can now be studied at the Campo Santo, Pisa, where war damage in 1945 by destroying the surface of the great fescoes revealed the underlying original underpaintings, the so-called *Sinopie*.

6 *White of egg. (Glaire) Eyger Clor*

The word *eyger clor* means simply white of egg but when the German term is used to denote the prepared painting medium made from white of egg, it is translated as glaire.

Glaire for painting is made as follows: Put the white of an egg in a basin and beat it up with a whisk until the froth is so stiff that you can turn the basin up-side-down without the froth moving. Next pour over the beaten-up white three quarters of a tumbler of water and leave the mixture to stand overnight, the froth is then removed and the liquid is ready for use. In this Manuscript is to be found on page 29 another way of making glaire which may have been quicker than the receipt given above but would seem to be neither such a good nor so clean a process. *N.B.* Glaire made for use as a varnish was beaten up without the addition of water. See Cennini's *Trattato*.

7 *Lye. Lougen*

A potash water produced by boiling finely sifted wood ash or ash from all sorts of plants with the addition of a small quantity of quick-lime. In this case it may even have been lye made with wood ash and water alone.

8 *Saffron. Saffrans*

The petals and stigmas of these flowers dried and crushed to powder were much used as a dye as also for a colour prized by illuminators. The colour was sometimes extracted by water alone, but vinegar or gum was also used in some cases.

⁹ *Brun*

Das Wort *brun* scheint entweder einen tiefen oder einen warmen Farbton bezeichnet zu haben.

¹⁰ *Opiment*

Ein Gelb, das häufig von mittelalterlichen Malern verwendet wurde, aber jetzt praktisch unerhältlich ist. Siehe Cennini's *Trattato*.

¹¹ 1 *Lot*

Man weiss, dass das Gewicht von einem Lot etwa das Äquivalent von $\frac{1}{2}$ oz. ist. Andere Maassangaben in der Übersetzung können aber nur als ungefähre akzeptiert werden, da es schwierig ist, sie über diese lange Zeitspanne hinweg einwandfrei festzulegen. In einigen Fällen, wo das entsprechende englische Maass nicht zu ermitteln war, wurde das alte deutsche Wort in den Text aufgenommen.

¹² *Bresil Holz*

Es wird auch *persilin, persil, prisil* etc. buchstabiert.

Eine schöne rosa Farbe wurde aus Splittern oder Hobelspänen dieses mahagony-farbigen Holzes gewonnen. Wenn man es mit Lauge, Alaun oder mit beidem kocht, so erhält man ein glühendes Rot mit etwas verschiedenen Schattierungen, gemass den Beifügungen während der Herstellung.

Der Name Brazil rührt von dem Wort Brazilin her, dem wesentlichen in dem Holz enthaltenen Farbstoff; er hat nichts mit dem Land Brasilien zu tun. Siehe *Materials of Medieval Painting*, D. V. Thompson, und Chamber's Encyclopaedia.

¹³ *Glas*

Das Wort *Glas* bedeutet hier wahrscheinlich ein Wasser-Glas, an andern Stellen aber scheint es Glasflasche zu bedeuten.

¹⁴ *Wassers von Winstein*

Das tartarum, Weinstein, war wahrscheinlich nicht flüssig, da die Menge mit einem trockenen Maass angegeben wird, z. B. "die Grösse einer Erbse". Das Wort "Wassers" mag darauf hindeuten, dass der Weinstein so floss wie Sand in einem Stundenglass. In Gerarde's *Herball* wird Weinstein in folgender Weise beschrieben: "Der Bodensatz von Wein, der so hart wie eine Kruste geworden ist, . . . er ist trocken, hart, fest und sehr dicht und kann zu Pulver gerieben werden; in den Läden wird er Tartarum genannt, auf Englisch Argall und Tartar . . . ; die Silber-schmiede polieren ihr Silber damit . . . , die Färber benutzen ihn . . . , er hat durchaus bindende Eigenschaften . . . Dieser Bodensatz wird manchmal gebrannt: wenn er dann ganz weiss wird, so ist das ein Beweis der richtigen und perfekten Art des Brennens, und die Apotheker bezeichnen es mit Tartarum ustum oder Tartarum calcinatum. Es schmilzt . . . wenn es in einem leinenen Säckchen in einem Keller unter der Erde aufgehängt wird.

¹⁵ *Röth bi truken*

Die Phrase sollte wahrscheinlich heissen: *Gar röthli truken*. Das würde bedeuten, dass die Farbe ganz trocknen sollte, damit man feststellen konnte, ob sie die erwünschte Nüance habe. (Siehe Anmerkung ¹).

Deep. Brun
The word *brun* appears to have meant either deep or warm in tone.

Orpiment. Opiment
A yellow in frequent use by medieval painters but now practically unobtainable.
See Cennini's *Trattato*.

$\frac{1}{2}$ *oz.* 1 *Lot*
The weight of a lot is known to be equivalent to $\frac{1}{2}$ oz. Other measures given in the
translation, however, must be considered to be only approximate as it is difficult
to establish anything definite at this distance of time. In some cases where the
English equivalent is not ascertainable the old German word is used in the English
text.

Brazilwood. Bresil Holtz, also spelt *persilin, persil, prisil,* etc.
A beautiful rose colour was made from the chips or shavings of this mahogany
coloured wood. Boiled with lye or with alum or both of these it yields a glowing red
of slightly differing hues according to the additive used in the making.
　　The name Brazil comes from the word brazilin, the essential dye stuff contained
in the wood and not from any reference to the country Brazil. See *Materials of
Medieval Painting,* D. V. Thompson; also Chambers's *Encyclopaedia.*

Glass. Glas
The word *glas* here probably means a glass tumbler but in other places it would
appear to mean a glass bottle.

Tartarum. Wassers von Winstein
The *tartarum* was presumably not in a liquid state as the amount given is a dry
measure, i.e. 'the size of a pea'. The word 'wassers' may suggest that the tartar was
fluid like sand in an hour-glass; in Gerarde's *Herball* tartarum is described as
follows: 'The lees of wine which is become hard like a crust . . . being dry hard
sound and well compact and which may be beaten into a powder called in shops
Tartarum in English Argall and Tartar . . . the silversmiths polish their silver with
it . . . the Diers use it . . . it hath withal a binding facultie . . . This lees is often times
burnt: if it become all white it is a signe of right and perfect burning the Apothe-
caries call it Tartarum ustum and Tartarum calcinatum. It melteth . . . if it be
hanged in a linen bagge in some place in a cellar under the ground'.

A good Red. Röth bi truken
The phrase should probably read *gar röthli truken.* This would indicate that the
colour should be left to dry in order to see if it were the shade required. (see Note1).

und . . .
"tu" muss hier nach dem Wort *und* ausgelassen worden sein.

¹⁷ *Fundament*
Dies ist die erhabene Oberfläche, die die Illuminierer für grosse Buchstaben und andere Ornamente auf Kalbspergament und Pergament benutzten, und die vergoldet und danach poliert wurden.

In den Handbüchern italienischer Maler wird dies *assiso* genannt, und diese Bezeichnung wird noch oft benutzt.

¹⁸ *Nass*
Diese Answeisungen bedeuten nicht, dass die Oberfläche nicht trocken darf, sondern dass sie nach dem Trocknen mit einem nassen Pinsel und mit demselben Mittel angefeuchtet werden soll wie bei der Applikation von Blattgold auf eine vorbereitete Fläche.

¹⁹ *Truken*
Dieses wie das folgende Rezept behandeln die trockene Methode des Vergoldens. Sie unterscheidet sich von der nassen Methode insofern, als die erhabene Oberfläche nicht wieder angefeuchtet wird, bevor das Blattgold appliziert wird. Die kleine Menge Honig, die man der Goldmischung hinzufügte, wurde als genügend betrachtet, um die Oberfläche gerade klebrig genug zu halten, damit das Gold an ihr haftete, wenn es lediglich angepresst wurde, oder auch nach Anhauchen leicht hineingedrückt wurde.

²⁰ *heideschen Ziegel*
Für die Zubereitung einer Grundierung für Blattgold wäre eine Substanz wie pulverisierter Ziegelstein völlig ungeeignet. Man kann daher annehmen, dass mit *heideschen Ziegel* eine der vielen fein pulverisierten Erden gemeint ist, die von Goldschmieden benutzt wurden, wie Bleicherde.

Die letztere wurde auch *Terra sigillata* genannt, (siehe *Art of Fresco Painting*, Mrs. Merrifield). Man kann daher annehmen, dass *Ziegel* eine Entstellung von Siegel ist, in welchem Fall das Wort *heideschen* ursprünglich *feinesten* gewesen sein mag. Derartige Fehler können in der gothischen Schrift noch leichter unterlaufen als in der lateinischen, wie jeder, der sich die Mühe gibt, die fraglichen Worte in gothisch auszuschreiben, bezeugen kann.

²¹ *Aurum Musitum*
Ein künstliches Gelb, das Gold vortäuschen sollte. Der Name erscheint in manchen Manuskripten als *Aurum Musicum* und im *Trattato* als *Porporina*. Cennini sagt, es sei eine Farbe, die wie Gold aussieht und sich gut zum Miniaturmalen auf Pergament eignet, doch warnt er davor, sie mit wirklichem Gold in Berührung kommen zu lassen.

²² *bletter*
Im Mittelalter war Blattgold fast doppelt so dick wie das heutzutage benutzte Gold, daher sollte die angegebene Menge von Goldblättern verdoppelt werden, wenn das Experiment mit diesem Rezept erfolgreich sein soll.

¹⁶ *And take. und . . .*
'Tu' must have been left out here, after the word *und*.

¹⁷ *Foundation. Fundament*
This is the illuminators raised ground for capital letters and other ornamentations on vellum and parchment which are to be gilded and afterwards burnished.

In the Italian painters manuals it is called *assiso* and this term is still often used.

¹⁸ *Wet Method. Nass*
The directions here do not mean that the foundation must not be allowed to dry but that after drying it should be damped with a wet brush in the same manner and with the same medium as that in which gold leaf is applied to a prepared panel.

¹⁹ *Dry Method. Truken*
In this as in the following receipt the dry method of gilding is alluded to. It differs from the wet method in that the foundation is not to be made damp again before the gold leaf is applied. The small amount of honey which was to be put in the gold size would be sufficient to keep the surface just tacky enough to allow of the leaf adhering by being merely pressed down or alternatively by being breathed upon and lightly pressed home.

²⁰ *Lemnian Earth. heideschen Ziegel*
For the purpose of making a foundation for gold leaf, any substance such as brick dust would be totally unsuitable. It must be concluded therefore, that by *heideschen Ziegel* is meant one of the many finely powdered earths used by goldsmiths; such as fullers earth, Tripoli sand or Lemnian earth. The last of these is also called *Terra sigillata* (sealed earth) (see *Art of Fresco Painting* by Mrs. Merrifield). It might therefore be conjectured that *Ziegel* represents a misspelling of *Siegel* (German for seal) in which case the word *heideschen* might have originally been *feinesten*. Mistakes of this kind would be even easier to make in the gothic script than in a Roman hand as anyone who cares to write out the words in question in the former script can prove.

²¹ *Mosaic Gold. Aurum Musitum*
An artificial yellow used to simulate gold. Its name appears in some manuscripts as *Aurum Musicum* and in the *Trattato* under that of *Porporina*. Cennini calls it a colour like gold, and he says it is a good colour for miniature painters on parchment, but warns against its being allowed to touch real gold.

²² *Leaves. bletter*
In the middle ages gold leaf was almost double the thickness of the standard leaf used today. Therefore twice the number of leaves mentioned should be used if the experiment in this receipt is to be successful.

23 *Wasser*

Dies ist wahrscheinlich das zweite Mittel, das bei den *zwei edli guti wassers*, die auf Seite 42 erwähnt sind, fehlt, und wo nur eines angegeben wird. Die Tatsache, dass beide in ähnlicher Weise beginnen und dass beide mit der Bemerkung schliessen, dass das Bindemittel die Beschaffenheit von Öl haben sollte, scheint diese Annahme zu unterstützen.

24 *Badstein*

Dies ist wahrscheinlich ein Schreibfehler, anstelle von *badslein*, wörtlich Bade-Leinentuch. Es ist nicht das einzige Mal, dass in diesem Manuskript St und L miteinander verwechselt worden sind. Die Art der Verwendung von *badstein* schliesst es aus, dass man sich hier auf irgendeine Art von Stein bezogen hat. Andererseits ist es möglich, dass das Wort *badstein* Schwamm bedeutete. Siehe Rezept für Bereitung von Eiweissfarbe, (Napels Codex).

25 *Tüchlin*

Die in italienischen Manuscripten *pezzuoli* oder *pezzuli* genannten Wasserfarben, und 'Clothlet' oder 'Ragge' colours in alt-englischen Manualen wurden weitgehend zum Färben und Illuminieren verwendet. Siehe Lyte's *Botany* 1578. Sie waren ihrer Natur nach durchsichtig und ziemlich substanzlos. In ihnen wurden kleine Leintücher für Aufbewahrungszwecke gefärbt. Waschblau, das man zum Bleichen von Leinen verwendete, war wahrscheinlich ein überlebender Rest dieser Färbe-tüchlein-Tradition.

26 *Varwe*

Das Wort blau scheint hier ausgelassen worden zu sein. Späterhin wird ein Rezept für die Gewinnung von blau aus den Blütenblättern blauer Blumen gegeben, das in gleicher Weise hergestellt wird; die Blumen hierfür werden zu Pfingsten ge-pflückt. Ein anderes Rezept für rosa Kornblumen ist diesem sehr ähnlich, nur ist das sal ammoniac weggelassen. So gewinnt man eine lila Farbe. In einem vierten, etwas andersartigem Rezept werden sowohl die Farbe, blau, als auch die Blumen, Kornblumen, erwähnt, und in allen vier Rezepten ist die erwähnte Zeit für das Pflücken die Pfingstzeit, oder es wird gesagt "um dieselbe Zeit des Jahres". Man wusste, dass Kornblumen, *cyanus flos*, eine strahlend blaue Flüssigkeit enthalten.

27 7

Die Bezeichnung in dem deutschen Manuskript ist kaum zu verstehen; aber sie kann unmöglich nur 7 Kornblumen bedeuten. Berger ist der Ansicht, dass 7 Hände voll gemeint sind, und als Bestätigung folgt der Anzahl 17 auf Seite 36 in einem ähnlichen Rezept das Wort *hantvol*. Augenscheinlich war die Quantität der benutzten Blumen nicht genau festgelegt, da in diesen Rezepten für Kornblumen die Quantität von Alaun etc. sich gemäss der Menge der gesammelten Blumen zu ändern hat.

28 *Zit*

— Pfingstzeit.

Dieses Wort ist von grossem Wert für die Feststellung, dass die vier erwähnten Rezepte sämtlich aus dem Saft von Kornblumen zubereitet wurden.

29 *Mürsel*

Die fehlende Phrase mag folgenderweise gelautet haben: *Bereit sei und stosse sie*, gleichbedeutend mit "Wenn sie bereit sind, zerstosse man sie".

²³ *Medium. Wasser*

This is possibly the second medium which is missing from the *Zwei edli guti wassers* alluded to on page 42 where only one is given. The fact that both begin in much the same manner and that they both end with the remark that the medium should be of the consistency of oil would seem to support this view.

[23] *Medium. Wasser*
This is possibly the second medium which is missing from the *Zwei edli guti wassers* alluded to on page 42 where only one is given. The fact that both begin in much the same manner and that they both end with the remark that the medium should be of the consistency of oil would seem to support this view.

[24] *Linen Towel. Badstein*
This is possibly a slip for *badslein*, literally—bath linen. It is not the only place in the manuscript where 'st' and 'l' have been confused. The purpose for which the *badstein* is to be used rules out the possibility of any kind of stone being referred to. On the other hand, it is possible that the word *badstein* meant 'sponge'. See receipt for preparing glaire in the Naples Codex.

[25] *Rag. Tüchlin*
These water colours called *pezzuoli* or *pezzuli* in the Italian manuscripts and 'clothlet' or 'ragge' colours in the Old English manuals were widely used for dyeing and illuminating, see Lyte's *Botany*, 1578. They were of their nature transparent and without much substance and were kept, for storage purposes, dyed into small pieces of linen rag. Blue bag used for whitening linen was possibly a survival of clothlet tradition.

[26] *Colour. Varwe*
The word blue seems to have been missed out here. There is a receipt further on for making blue from the petals of blue flowers which is made in an identical manner, the flowers being picked at Whitsuntide. Another receipt for pink cornflowers is much the same except that the sal ammoniac is left out. This makes a violet. In a fourth receipt, of a slightly different nature both the colour—blue—and the flowers—cornflowers are mentioned, and in all four receipts the time of year for picking is mentioned at Whitsuntide, or else as at the 'same time of year'. Cornflowers, *cyanus flos*, are known to contain a bright blue liquid.

[27] *A Quantity. 7*
The mark '7' in the German script is difficult to understand but it cannot mean just seven cornflowers. Berger takes it to denote seven handfuls and certainly on page 36 in a similar receipt the number 17 is followed by the word *hantvol*. Evidently no precise amount of flowers is referred to as in these receipts for cornflowers the quantity of alum, etc. is to be varied according to the amount of flowers gathered.

[28] *Time of Year. Zit*
Whitsuntide—
This word is most valuable in helping to identify that the four receipts in question were all made from the juice of cornflowers.

[29] *Mortar. Mürsel*
The missing passage may have run as follows—*bereit sei und stosse sie* 'are ready then crush them'.

[30] . . . *gat in*

In diesem Satz sind die Worte *die varwe* offensichtlich ausgelassen worden.

[31] *die* . . .

Das Wort *rötin* (roter Farbstoff) fehlt hier offensichtlich.

[32] *Ziegelstein*

Eine absorbierende Fläche wäre erforderlich, um den Farbstoff gründlich austrocknen zu lassen. Poröse Platten werden jetzt noch benutzt, um den Niederschlag auszutrocknen. Siehe *De arte illuminandi* übersetzt von D. V. Thompson.

[33] *Lagga*

Mittelalterliche Lacke stammten aus verschiedenen Quellen, und man sollte sie von den Krapplacken einer späteren Periode unterscheiden. Der hier erwähnte Lack ist wahrscheinlich der indische Gummi-Lack, der in grossem Maass von Venedig eingeführt wurde. Cennini erwähnt, dass der beste Lack "Aus einem dunklen Gummi, der trocken und körnig ist", hergestellt wurde, aber man weiss nicht, ob er sich auf den indischen Lack bezog, siehe *Materials for Medieval Painting*, D. V. Thompson.

[34] *Megdenbermenten*

Das moderne deutsche Wort Pergament gilt für die beiden englischen Bezeichnungen parchment und vellum; und die alten Worte *berment*, *bermenten* und *bermit* wurden wahrscheinlich in gleicher Weise benutzt. Wo *Megdenberment* gesagt wird, bezeichnet es Pergament aus Kalbshaut. Miss Dorothy Hutton ist der Ansicht, dass Pergament aus Kalbshaut in frühen Zeiten häufiger für gemalte Manuskripte benutzt wurde als gewöhnliches Pergament.

[35] *Schlecht*

Das Wort *schlecht* kann hier nicht die Bedeutung haben, die es im modernen Deutsch hat; es scheint mehr Ähnlichkeit mit dem deutschen Wort *schlicht* zu haben, im Sinne von glatt oder eben. Siehe auch Seite 42, wo es zur Beschreibung eines dünnen fliessenden Öles benutzt wird.

[36] *Roten Blumen*

Der Name der Blumen fehlt unglücklicherweise. Ernst Berger in seinen *Beiträge* meint, es könnten Päonien sein, aber es ist ungewiss, ob man diese in genügenden Mengen gefunden hätte. Es ist wahrscheinlicher, dass es wilde Mohnblumen waren, — *Papava eraticum*, auch *Papava rubrum* und *Papava Rhea* genannt, die man fast überall in Nordeuropa in grossen Mengen finden kann. Wenn man die Blütenblätter von scharlachroten Mohnblumen mit Alaun kocht, erhält man eine bläulichlila Farbe.

[37] *Lamptschen Sitte.*
Siehe Anmerkung [42].

[38] *Gans eij*

Das Wort *gans* bedeutet auch 'das Ganze'; diese Phrase kann also bedeuten 'Benutze die Menge eines ganzen Eies'. Aber in Büchern aus jener Zeit und selbst aus noch späteren Perioden wird die Grösse eines Gänse-Eies manchmal als Mengenmaass angegeben. So in Gerard's *Herbal* 1698, wo es sich auf die Grösse von Tomaten bezieht, die damals *love apples* genannt wurden.

³⁰ *The colour goes into . . . gat in*
In this sentence the words *die varve* have evidently been left out.

³¹ *The red colouring matter. die . . .*
The word *rötin* (red colouring matter) is evidently missing here.

³² *Tile. Ziegelstein*
An absorbent surface would be required to allow the pigment to dry thoroughly. Porous plates are still used to dry out precipitates. See *De arte illuminandi* übersetzt von D. V. Thompson.

³³ *Lac (Lake). Lagga*
Medieval lakes came from several sources and are to be distinguished from the madder lakes of a later period. The lac mentioned here is probably the gum lac of India much imported from Venice. Cennini in the *Trattato* mentions that the best kind of lac was made from 'a dark gum which is dry and granular' but it is not known whether he was referring to the Indian lac, see *The Materials of Medieval Painting*, D. V. Thompson.

³⁴ *Vellum. Megdenbermenten*
The modern German word *pergament* includes both parchment and vellum, and the old terms *berment, bermenten,* and *bermit* were probably used in the same way. Where *megdenbermenten* appears it denotes vellum. According to Miss Dorothy Hutton vellum, i.e. calf skin, was more often used than ordinary parchment for illuminated manuscripts in early times.

³⁵ *Flat. Schlecht*
Obviously the word *schlecht* cannot here mean bad as in modern German but appears to have closer affinity to the German word *schlict* sleek or smooth, etc. See also page 42 where it is used to describe a thin and flowing oil.

³⁶ *Red Flowers. Roten Blumen*
The name of the flowers is unfortunately missing. Ernst Berger in his *Beiträge* suggests they may be peonies but it is doubtful if these would have been found in sufficient quantities. It seems more likely that they were wild poppies—*Papava eraticum* also called *Papava rubrum* and *Papava Rhea*, which would be found in large quantities almost everywhere in northern Europe. The petals of scarlet poppies when boiled with alum have been found to yield a bluish violet colour.

³⁷ *London Practice. Lamptschen Sitte*
See Note ⁴².

³⁸ *Goose egg. Gans eij*
The word *gans* also means entirely, so the passage might mean 'Take up the amount of a whole egg'. But in books of that time and indeed of an even later period the size of a goose egg is sometimes given as a quantity. It appears in *Gerarde's Herball* 1598 relating to the size of tomatoes, then called love apples.

[39] *Seken*

Der Buchstabe "t" scheint irrtümlicherweise ausgelassen worden zu sein. Das Wort sollte zweifellos *steken* heissen. Stöcke wurden und werden jetzt noch manchmal zum gründlichen Auswringen von Papierbrei benutzt.

[40] *Gebuchet*

Ein Fehler; wahrscheinlich anstatt *geblichet*, was gebleicht bedeutet. Siehe auch Berger's *Beiträge*.

[41] *Ander besser gesmak*

Die Übersetzung zwischen den Worten *vil* und *gesmak* kann aus der Tatsache abgeleitet werden, dass die Farben trocken gehalten werden mussten, um sie in gutem Zustand zu erhalten.

[42] *Ze Paris und ze lampten*

Unter Fachleuten bestehen ernste Meinungsverschiedenheiten über die Bedeutung des Wortes *lampten*, das hier immer mit London übersetzt wird. Sir Charles Eastlake ist in seinen *Materials for a History of Oil Painting* der Ansicht, dass es London bedeutet und bringt fast unwiderlegliche Beweise für seine Ansicht vor. Ernst Berger stellt jedoch in seinen *Beiträge* die Behauptung auf, dass *lampten* die Bedeutung von Lombardei hätte, und dass Eastlake durch patriotische Gründe, wie Berger meint, verleitet wurde, falsche Schlüsse zu ziehen. Dennoch scheint die Gegenüberstellung von Paris und London das stärkste Argument zugunsten von Eastlake's Ansicht zu sein; da es wahrscheinlicher ist, dass eine Stadt im Zusammenhang mit einer andern Stadt erwähnt wird, als eine Stadt im Zusammenhang mit einer Provinz.

[43] *Vor misal*

Den Worten *vor misal* wurde seltsamerweise von Ernst Berger in seinen *Beiträge* die Bedeutung *Tornesol* gegeben, aber die Farbe Tornesol wurde aus den Samen der gleichnamigen Pflanze gewonnen, und nicht, wie in diesem Rezept, aus den Blütenblättern von Kornblumen. Mit Bezug auf Tornesol finden wir in Lyte's *English Botany* 1578 folgende Auskunft: 'Mit den Samen der kleinen Tornesolpflanze färbt man alte Leinenlappen und Tücher purpurrot'. In Holmes' *Armoury* 1688 heisst es: 'An den Blättern bilden sich drei Beeren, in deren Innerem sich Tornesol zur Herstellung von Purpurrot entwickelt'. Siehe *The Materials of Medieval Painting*, D. V. Thompson. Gerarde's *Herball* gibt weitere Aufklärungen hierüber, indem es sagt: 'Sie sind bisher in England noch unbekannt; sie wachsen in der Gegend von Montpelier im Languedoc, wo sie in grossen Mengen zum Färben und Einfärben von Lappen benutzt werden' . . . 'mit der kleinen Tornesol färben sie in Frankreich Leinentücher und Lappen in ein Vollendetes Purpurrot; solche Lappen werden in den Läden nach dem Namen der Pflanze Tornesol genannt'. Die Farbe Tornesol wurde oft mit Alaun versetzt, um eine blaue Schattierung zu erzeugen, aber diese Färbung war nicht dauerhaft, während das hier als *vor misal* und *tuchlin Blau* erwähnte Blau besonders deshalb empfohlen wird, weil diese Farbe 'für wenigstens 20 Jahre nicht verbleicht', selbst wenn sie nur in Gestalt des gefärbten Tuches aufgehoben wird.

³⁹ *Sticks. Seken*
The letter 't' seems to have been left out by mistake. The word should doubtless read *steken*. Sticks were and still are sometimes used to wring out pulp very thoroughly.

⁴⁰ *Bleached. Gebuchet*
A slip possibly, for *geblichet*, meaning bleached. See also Berger's *Beiträge*.

⁴¹ *Sweet and clean. Ander besser gesmak*
Between the words *vil* and *gesmak* the translation is conjectural from the fact that the colours would need to be kept dry to preserve them in good condition.

⁴² *In Paris and London. ze Paris und ze lampten*
There is a serious divergence of opinion between experts as to the meaning of the word *lampten* which is here always translated London. Sir Charles Eastlake in his *Materials for a History of Oil Painting* takes it to mean London and makes out an almost unanswerable case for this rendering. Ernst Berger, however in his *Beiträge* contends that *lampten* should be taken to mean Lombardy and that Eastlake was mistaken being swayed 'by patriotic motives' as he puts it, into coming to a wrong conclusion.

However the juxtaposition of Paris and London would seem to offer the strongest possible argument in favour of Eastlake's view, it being more probable that a town would be mentioned with another town rather than a town with a province.

⁴³ *Blue for Missals. Vor misal*
Strangely enough these words *vor misal* were taken to mean *Tornesol* by Ernst Berger in his *Beiträge*, but the colour Tornesol was made from the seeds of the plant of that name and not, as in this receipt from the petals of cornflowers. In relation to Tornesol, we find in Lyte's *English Botany* 1578 the following information 'with the seede of the small Tornesol they die and staine old linnen cloutes and ragges into a purple colour'. In Holmes' *Armoury* 1688 it says 'at the leaves come forth three berries which have within them of which that Tournesol is made purple colour'. See *The Materials of Medieval Painting*, D. V. Thompson. Gerarde's *Herball* 1597 gives further light on the subject and says 'They are strangers in Englande as yet, it doth growe about Montpelier in Languedoc where it is had in great use to staine and die clouts withal . . . with the small tornesole they in France do die linnen rags and clouts into a perfect purple colour which clouts in shops be called Tornesol after the name of the herbe'. The colour tornesol was often treated with alum to give it a blue shade but this tint was not permanent, whereas the blue mentioned here as *vor misal* and *tuchlin Blau* is expressly recommended as keeping its colour 'for at least twenty years' even while only stored in the rag.

H

44 *Substancie*

Das etwas seltsame Wort *substancie* mag seine Erklärung in der Tatsache finden, dass das italienische Wort *sostanza* unter anderm auch Kern bedeutet. Auch in Gerarde's *Herball* wird das englische Wort 'substance' gleichbedeutend wie harter Kern oder Kern benutzt. Man kann daher wohl folgern, dass, da Galläpfel bekanntlich zur Tintegewinnung benutzt wurden und ihrer Natur nach einen harten inneren Kern haben, sie der erwähnte Bestandteil sind. Gerarde unterscheidet zwischen Galls und oak apples, indem er sagt, 'Oke apples sind den gals sehr ähnlich jedoch sind sie von schlechterer Qualität und weniger kräftig'.

45 *Lampenschen Sitten*

Siehe Anmerkung [42].

46 *Rot Blau*

Dies bedeutet wahrscheinlich, dass sowohl warme als auch kalte durchsichtige Farben beschrieben worden sind, nicht nur rote und blaue.

47 *Zwei*

Hier wird nur ein Rezept für Wasserfarben-Bindemittel angegeben. Es ist möglich, dass das zweite erwähnte Rezept sich auf Seite 29 befindet, siehe Anmerkung [23]. Es war durchaus nicht unüblich, dass sich ein Blatt aus einem Manuskript irgendwann loslöste und später an einer verkehrten Stelle wieder eingefügt wurde.

48 *Zinober*

Das Wort Zinober ist hier offenbar irrtümlich anstelle von *ze bulver* benutzt worden, wie sich aus dem Zusammenhang ergibt. Siehe auch Berger's *Beiträge*.

49 *Lamptschen Endaco*

Dies soll wohl Färberwaid-Indigo bedeuten, zum Unterschied von der indischen Art. Die Zusammenfassung von *Lamptschen* mit *endaco* ist ein weiterer Hinweis darauf, dass Lampten London bedeutet, denn es ist allgemein bekannt, dass Färberwaid (*Glastum*) in grossem Umfang in England angepflanzt wurde. Gerarde in seinem *Herball* schliesst seine Beschreibung der Pflanze: 'Sie eignet sich sehr gut zum Durchfärben und Färben von Stoff, was für wenige einträglich und für viele von Nachteil ist'. Siehe Amnerkung [41]. Dies ist eine Anspielung auf den Kraftverlust, den der Boden durch den Anbau dieser Pflanze erlitt, was auch beweist, dass sie vielfach angepflanzt wurde.

50 *Harvarwe*

Erst nach vier Rezepten, die sich mit der Zubereitung verschiedener Farben beschäftigen, wird das Thema Haar wieder eingeführt. Am Ende des Rezeptes für Saftgrün scheint der Text etwas verwirrt zu sein, da dem Studenten abrupt und ohne jede Erklärung gesagt wird, 'eine Lage hiervon mit Gummi Arabicum über das Haar zu breiten'.

51 *Licht Blau Lazur*

Wahrscheinlich bedeutet dieser Ausdruck Himmelblau, das auch *azzuro della magna* genannt wird, da diese Farbe häufig in Nordeuropa benutzt wurde.

44 *Oak Apples. Substancie*
Light is thrown on this rather curious word *substancie* by the fact that one of the meanings of the Italian word *sostanza*—substance, is kernel. Again in Gerarde's *Herball* the English word 'substance' is used as synonymous with hard core or kernel. It may well be inferred therefore that as oak apples are known to have been used for ink and have of their nature a hard inside core that they are the ingredient referred to. Gerarde distinguishes between gals and oak apples saying, 'Oke apples are much of the same nature as gals, yet are they farre inferior unto them and of lesser force'.

45 *London Practice. Lampenschen Sitten*
See Note [42].

46 *Warm and Cold. Rot Blau*
This probably means that the transparent colours both warm and cold have been described, not just reds and blues.

47 *Two. Zwei*
One receipt only for a water colour medium is given here. It is possible that the second one referred to is that to be found on page 29. See Note [23]. There would be nothing unusual in a leaf from the Manuscript getting detached at some time, and later being put back in the wrong place.

48 *To powder. Zinober*
The word *zinober* here is evidently a slip for *ze bulver* as can be gathered from the context. See also Berger's *Beiträge*.

49 *London Indigo. Lamptschen Endaco*
Probably this means woad indigo as distinguished from the Indian kind. The combination of *Lamptschen* with *endaco* is a further indication that *Lampten* is to be identified with London, for it is well known that woad (*Glastum*) was much grown in England. Gerarde in his *Herball* ends his description of the plant with 'It serveth well to die and colour cloth, profitable to some few and hurtful to many'. See Note [42]. This alludes to the state of poverty in which the cultivation of this plant left the soil, also proving that it was much grown.

50 *Hair Colour. Harvarwe*
It is not till after four receipts on making up different colours that the subject of hair is again introduced. At the end of the receipt on sap green there appears to be some confusion as abruptly, without any explanation, the student is told to 'lay a coat of this with gum arabic over the hair'.

51 *Light Blue azurite. Licht Blau Lazur*
In all probability this means azurite blue otherwise called *azzuro della magna*, as this colour was much used in Northern Europe.

Hier werden drei Arten genannt. Die erste, 'veil-Beeren', ist wahrscheinlich nicht als Veilchen, sondern eher als gewöhnlicher Liguster (*Ligurtaum*), Rainweide auf deutsch, zu identifizieren; die zweite 'Buckthorn' (*Rhamnus*) wird in Gerard's *Herbal* erwähnt; er sagt: 'Aus den reifen Beeren wird ein Saft herausgepresst, der mit etwas Alaun gekocht wird und dann von Malern als ein Dunkelgrün benutzt wird, das sie Sap greene nennen'. Die dritte Beere ist höchstwahrscheinlich die von Dyers Greenweed, auf deutsch Ginster, *Genista Tinctoria*, deren Beeren gemäss Gerard zum Grünfärben benutzt wurden; er nennt die Pflanze *Diers greening weed*, *Base Broome* und *woodwaxen*.

53 *Ane Routh*
Die wörtliche Übersetzung hiervon ist ohne Mitleid, oder mitleidslos. Die Verbindung zwischen *routh* mit dem angelsächsischen Wort *ruthe* gleich Mitleid kann mit Leichtigkeit festgestellt werden.

54 *Lindes blottern*
Die Bedeutung hier ist wahrscheinlich Ochsenblase; daher sollten die Worte *linde blottern* heissen *rinde blottern*.

55 *Substancie*
Siehe Anmerkung [44].

56 *und . . . das*
Es scheint, als ob das Wort *Strich* ausgelassen worden ist; es sollte vor dem Wort "das" stehen, wie in dem Satz des vorhergehenden Rezepts.

57 *gar liecht blau har varve*
Dies ist wohl ein Fehler, anstelle von 'gar liecht blau varve'.

58 *Öliwis*
Wahrscheinlich ein Schreibfehler anstatt bliwis. Siehe die *Beiträge*, Ernst Berger.

59 *Varve*
Anstelle des Wortes 'varve' sollte wahrscheinlich Garn stehen; es wurde daher auch demgemäss übersetzt. Direkt hiernach werden Anweisungen für 'Garn' gegeben: das Garn gründlichst einzutauchen.

60 *Lin* (meist Lim buchstabiert)
Dieser äusserst wichtige Bestandteil von Malmaterialien wurde immer aus Pergamentschnitzeln hergestellt, aber dieses Rezept unterscheidet sich etwas von dem einfacheren Malrezept, das im *Trattato* angegeben wird. Diesem Rezept werden Essig und Honig hinzugefügt. Siehe *Trattato* und *Papers of the Society of Mural Decorators and Painters in Tempera*, Band II: P. Tudor Hart's Rezept für Grundieren. Siehe auch *Practical Tempera Painting*, Borradaile.

[52] *Berries. Ber*
Three kinds are here named. The first 'veil' berries are probably not those of the violet but are more likely identifiable with the common Privet (*Ligurtaum*) *Rainweide* in German; the second, Buckthorn (*Rhamnus*) is mentioned in Gerard's *Herbal*, he says, 'There is pressed forth of the ripe berries a juice which being boyled with a little Allum is used of painters for a deepe greene which they do call Sap greene'. The third berry is more than probably that of Dyer's Greenweed, *Genista Tinctoria*, the berries of which Gerard says were used as a green dye and calls the plant Diers greening weed, Base Broome and woodwaxen.

[53] *Continuously. Ane Routh*
The literal translation of this is *ane* (without), *routh* (pity or relentlessly). The connection between *routh* and the Anglo Saxon word *ruthe* (pity) can be readily traced.

[54] *Ox Bladder. Lindes blottern*
An ox bladder is probably the meaning here intended, so the words *linde blottern* should read *rinde blottern*.

[55] *Cores. Substancie*
See Note [44].

[56] *Paint it. und . . . das*
It seems that the word *strich* has been left out and should precede *das* as in the sentence in the foregoing receipt.

[57] *Very light blue. gar liecht blau har varve*
This is probably a mistake for *gar liecht blau varve*.

[58] *Leadwhite. Oliwis*
Most probably a slip for bliwis. See the *Beiträge*, E. Berger.

[59] *Yarn. varve*
The word *varve* should probably read *garn*, and has therefore been so translated. Directions are given immediately afterwards for *garn*, the yarn, to be thoroughly immersed.

[60] *Size. Lin* (mostly spelt Lim)
This most important ingredient of the craftsmans materials was always made with parchment clippings, but the receipt here differs a little from the simpler one to be used for painting given in the *Trattato* in that vinegar and honey were added. See the *Trattato* also *Papers of the Society of Mural Decorators and Painters in Tempera* Vol. II for P. Tudor Hart's receipt for size. See also *Practical Tempera Painting*, Borradaile.

Die ursprünglichen Worte waren wohl *vil wenig.* Es ist unwahrscheinlich, dass es 'vil' hiess, was viel bedeutet. In mittelalterlichen Rezepten wird häufig davor gewarnt, zuviel Honig in den Mischungen zu verwenden; die Hinzufügung einer grossen Menge würde die Fähigkeit einer Mischung, zu trocknen, verringern.

62 *Oli*

Im Mittelalter wurden verschiedene Methoden, Malöle auszutrocknen, angewandt. Die hier angegebenen sind typische Beispiele. Keines ist so einfach wie die von Cennini benutzte italienische Methode, die darin besteht, dass man das Öl für einige Wochen einfach in heisser Sonne in einer Schale erhitzt, die in eine Kupferschüssel gestellt wird. Siehe *Practical Tempera Painting*, gekürzte Ausgabe von P. Tudor Hart's Rezept für das durch Sonnenhitze bewirkte Klären von Leinöl. Siehe auch Eastlake's *Materials for a History of Oil Painting*.

63 *Galicen stein*

Eastlake ist der Ansicht, dass Galicen Stein *Zink Vitriol* dedeutet, das auch oft *Weisses Vitriol*, oder *Zink Sulphat* genannt wird.

64 *halber bri.*

Das moderne deutsche Wort *Brei* bedeutet eine weiche Paste, und *halber* wahrscheinlich hier 'halbwegs'. Siehe Berger's *Beiträge*, in denen eine etwas andere Übersetzung steht, aber eine, die mit Bezug auf die Beschaffenheit im Ganzen dasselbe bedeutet.

65 *Niemen*

Ein Schreibfehler anstelle von *minien.* Sie die *Beiträge.*

66 *Rüschelecht*

Ein anderer Name für 'red orpiment'. Siehe *Trattato.*

67 *ze—*

Man könnte annehmen, dass das Wort *hindrest* an der Stelle des Striches in der Abschrift stehen sollte: dass das Hineinmahlen des Firnis der letzte Vorgang in der Zuberereitung von Ölfarben sein würde.

68 *Grünen*

Wir neigen zu der Annahme, dass das Wort 'grünen' *grunden* sein sollte. Es kann kaum grün bedeuten, da hiernach Anweisungen folgen, dass man eine Grundierung auf eine Fläche bringe, um dann mit einer Auswahl von Farben, die darüber in verschiedenen Schattierungen angelegt werden, eine dem Regenbogen ähnliche Wirkung zu erzielen. Siehe Cennini in seiner Anmerkung über '*a changing drapery*'.

69 *Paris Rot*

Man vergleiche die hier angegebenen Anweisungen für Fleischfarbe mit denen im *Trattato*, wo der Brauch der Toskanischen Schule angeführt wird; diese gibt die Anweisung, dass das einzige zu verwendende Rot beim Mischen von Fleischfarbe Zinnober sein sollte.

⁶¹ *very little. vil*
The original term was most likely *vil wenig*. It is unlikely to have been *vil* meaning much. Warnings against using too much honey in mediums are often found in medieval receipts. A large quantity would lessen the siccative property of any mixture to which it was added.

⁶² *Oil. Oli*
Several methods of siccatizing oils for painting were used in the Middle Ages. Those found here are typical examples. None of them is as simple as the Italian method given by Cennini which consists in the oil being merely heated in hot sunshine for some weeks in a basin placed inside a copper bowl. See *Practical Tempera Painting* for abridged version of P. Tudor Hart's receipt for sun-clarifying linseed oil.

See also Eastlake's *Materials for a History of Oil Painting*.

⁶³ *Zinc Vitriol. Galicen Stein*
Eastlake takes *Galicen Stein* to mean zinc vitriol, often called white vitriol or sulphate of zinc.

⁶⁴ *Soft paste. halber bri*
The modern German word *brei* means paste or pulp and *halber* in all probability here means 'half-way towards'. See Berger's *Beiträge* for a slightly different rendering, but one which gives much the same meaning as to consistency.

⁶⁵ *Red Lead. Niemen*
A slip for *minien*. See the *Beiträge*.

⁶⁶ *Realgar. Rüschelecht.*
Another name for red orpiment. See the *Trattato*.

⁶⁷ *Finally. ze—*
It can be conjectured that the dash in the copy represents the word *hindrest* as the grinding-in of the varnish would be the last process in the preparation of oil colours.

⁶⁸ *Grounding. Grünen*
We suggest that the word *grünen* may be *grunden*. It can hardly mean green as the directions which follow are for laying a ground colour and then giving it a rainbow-like effect with a variety of colours used to shade over it.

See Cennini in his note on 'a changing drapery'.

⁶⁹ *Paris Red. Paris Rot*
Compare the method given here for flesh painting with that in the *Trattato* which gives the practice of the Tuscan school in directing that the only red to be used when mixing up flesh colour was vermilion.

107

70 Verger

Aus dem Zusammenhang ergibt sich, dass dies ein Fehler anstelle von *augen* zu sein scheint.

71 Stein verger

Steinverger war wahrscheinlich eine andere Bezeichnung für Ocker, das gewöhnlich 'vergers' genannt wurde. Es war aber wohl eine besondere Art von Ocker, und an den zwei Stellen, an denen es erwähnt wird, geht ihm das Adjektiv 'dunkel' voran.

72 ouch das har us

'Ouch' ist sehr wahrscheinlich ein Schreibfehler anstelle von 'strich'. 'Us strichen' bedeutet umreissen, und es kommt verschiedene Male im Text vor.

73 Zendal

Man kann hier aus dem Zusammenhang entnehmen, dass das als zendal geschriebene Wort 'Ziegel' sein sollte und Terracotta-Kacheln oder Ziegelsteine mitumfasst. Der Bindestrich am Ende dieses Wortes *zendal* im deutschen Text scheint auf eine Abkürzung des Wortes hinzuweisen und berechtigt zu der Annahme, dass das ganze Wort 'Ziegelstein' gewesen ist, wie auf Seite 34; doch scheint keine Endung zu dem Wort *zendal*, die durch einen Bindestrich angedeutet sein könnte, zu existieren.

74 werde . . .

Das fehlende Wort war wahrscheinlich *getränkt*, was in diesem Falle gründlich grundiert bedeuten würde.

75 Stein

Wir haben hier den endgültigen Beweis, dass man es für erforderlich hielt, dem Stein dieselbe vorbereitende Grundierung zu geben wie Holz und Stoffen. Den Beweis, dass auch Terracotta (siehe Anmerkung 73) zu dieser Gruppe gehört, findet man in Pacheco's *L'Arte de la Pintura*. Hier wird gesagt, dass Terracotta dieselbe Applikation von Grundierung benötigt wie Holz und Stein.

Für diejenigen, die die *Beiträge* studieren, mag der Hinweis von Wichtigkeit sein, dass ein böser Schreibfehler —, die Unterschiebung das Wortes *lein*, — in dem bezüglichen Paragraph zu einiger Verwirrung der Ansichten über die Vorbereitung von Steinoberflächen für Vergoldung geführt hat; trotz der Tatsache, dass an anderer Stelle in demselben Band die Liste der Materialien korrekt sagt: *Auf holtz, tuch oder stein.*

76 herti

Herti würde hier hart und nicht aufsaugend bedeuten, etwa wie Eisen; zum Unterschied von nur hart wie Stein, der eine aufsaugende Oberfläche hat.

77 mit Öli getränkt

Es kann als sehr wahrscheinlich angenommen werden, dass Öl hier Ölfarbe bedeutet, so wie wir von Malen in Öl sprechen. Die Tradition, Stein mit Öl und Bleiweiss, und gelegentlich mit Öl und Ocker zu grundieren, rührt aus frühen Zeiten. Man macht auch heute die Erfahrung, dass es für Vergolden auf Stein tatsächlich erforderlich ist, eine Lage von Ölfarbe auf die Steinoberfläche zu bringen, und zwar unter der Goldmischung, um eine vollständig glatte und ebene Oberfläche zu erhalten, auf die das Blattgold gelegt wird.

⁷⁰ *Eyes. Verger*
From the context, this appears to be a mistake for *augen* (eyes).

⁷¹ *Ochre. Stein verger*
Stein verger was presumably another name for ochre usually called *vergers*. It was probably a special variety however, and in the two places in which it is mentioned it is preceded by the adjective dark.

⁷² *Outline the hair. ouch das har us*
Ouch is most probably a slip for the word *strich*. *Us strichen* means to outline and occurs several times in the text.

⁷³ *Terracotta. Zendal —*
The context here suggests that the word appearing as '*zendal*'—(gauze) should be '*ziegel*' including terracotta, tile or brick. The hyphen appearing at the end of this word *zendal* in the German text seems to indicate a shortened form of word and suggests that the whole may have been '*ziegelstein*' as on page 34, whereas there appears to be no known suffix to the word *zendal* that a hyphen could represent.

⁷⁴ *is thoroughly sized. werde . . .*
The missing word was probably *getränkt* meaning in this case throughly sized.

⁷⁵ *Stone. Stein*
We here find conclusive evidence that stone was considered as requiring the same preliminary sizing as wood and fabric. Proof that terracotta (see Note ⁷³) would also have been included in this group is to be found in Pacheco's *L'Arte de la Pintura* where terracotta is described as needing the same application of size as wood and stone. To those studying the *Beiträge* it may be helpful to point out that an unfortunate slip—the substitution of the word *lein* in the paragraph under consideration—has led to a certain confusion of thought in connection with the preparation of stone surfaces for gilding; and this, in spite of the fact that in another passage in the same volume the list of materials is given correctly as: *Auf holtz tuch oder stein.*

⁷⁶ *Hard. herti*
Hard here would mean hard and inabsorbent like iron, in contradistinction to merely hard like stone which has an absorbent surface.

⁷⁷ *Coat of Oil. mit öli getränkt*
It can be taken as highly probable that oil here means oil paint, as when we speak of painting in oils. The tradition of oil and white lead, and occasionally oil and ochre as a priming for stone goes back to early times. Modern experience of gilding on stone bears out the fact that a coat of oil paint is required on stone under the gold size in order to produce a perfectly smooth and even surface on which to lay the gold leaf.

[78] *Gemeine Virnis*
Dies war wahrscheinlich 'Sandaric resin' für das *Glassa* ein anderer Name war. Mastix wurde oft benutzt, aber war wohl kostbarer. Siehe Die *Schedula* von Theophilus.

[79] *Als vil*
Als vil mag auch bedeuten 'so viel' Knochenpulver, wie sich aus einem ganzen Knöchel gwinnen lässt.

[80] *Pappir*
Dies ist offensichlich eine Liste von Überschriften für eine Gruppe von Rezepten, von denen keines im deutschen Text enthalten ist. Die Tatsache, dass sie fehlen, macht es eindeutig klar, dass bereits Teile des Manuskriptes verlorengegangen waren, bevor die Abschrift im letzten Jahrhundert gemacht wurde.

[81] *Gold Varve*
Dies scheint dieselbe Mischung zu sein wie das Resept auf Seite 61, mit der Ausnahme, dass kleinere Mengen angegeben sind und dass die Goldmischung als letzte Vorbereitung gesiebt werden soll.

[82] *Aleo epaticum*
Siehe Ernst Berger's Anmerkung über *Goldgrundgummi* in die *Beiträge*.

[83] *Es folgt hier:*
Dieser Paragraph, der nur aus einer Liste von Überschriften besteht, die auf das Vergolden verschiedenartiger Oberflächen Bezug haben, scheint zum Teil I zu gehören, (siehe Seite 25), wo er eine Einleitung zu den Rezepten für Vergoldung bilden würde.

[84] *ein krut*
Das deutsche Wort Blutcrut deutet auf die Pflanze *Bloodwort* hin, über die Gerarde in seinem *Herball* sagt: 'Bloodwort ist im Lateinischen *Lapatum Sanguinem* . . . von blutroter Farbe, von der die ganze Pflanze erfüllt ist, sie ist das wichtigste under den Küchenkräutern'.

[85] *Wie man*
Hier haben wir wieder eine Reihe von Überschriften, die von den Rezepten, zu denen sie gehören, getrennt worden sind. Diese Rezepte selbst sind an verschiedenen Stellen des Manuskriptes zu finden.

⁷⁸ *Ordinary Varnish. Gemeine Virnis*
This was most probably Sandarac Resin, for which *glassa* was another name. Mastic resin was often used, but was probably more precious. See the *Schedula* by Theophilus.

⁷⁹ *As much as you require? Als vil*
Als vil might also mean 'as much' bone dust as a whole knuckle bone would yield.

⁸⁰ *Paper. Pappir*
This is evidently a list of headings to a group of receipts none of which are given in the German text. The fact that they are missing makes it clear that before the transcription was made during the last century, portions of the Manuscript had been lost.

⁸¹ *Gold Size. Gold Varwe*
This appears to be the same mixture as the receipt on page 61 except that smaller quantities are given and that the gold size is to be strained as a final preparation.

⁸² *Aleo hepaticum—Aleo epaticum*
See Ernst Berger's footnote on *Goldgrundgummi* in the *Beiträge*.

⁸³ *Here follows: Es folgt hier*
This paragraph being only a list of headings concerned with gilding on various surfaces would appear to belong to part 1 (see page 25) where it would form an introduction to the receipts on gilding.

⁸⁴ *A plant. ein krut*
The German word Blutcrut suggests that the plant is *Bloodwort* of which Gerarde in his *Herball* says 'Blood wort . . . is called in Latin *Lapatum Sanguinem* . . . of the bloodie colour wherewith the whole plant is possest, and is of potherbes the chief or principall'.

⁸⁵ *How one. Wie man*
Here again appears a set of headings which have been separated from the receipts to which they belong. These receipts themselves can be found in various places in the Manuscript.

BIBLIOGRAPHY / LITERATUR

BERGER, Ernst, *Quellen und Technik der Fresko-, Oel- und Tempera-Malerei des Mittelalters* . . . Bearbeitet von E. Berger. (Bd. 3. Beiträge zur Entwicklungs-Geschichte der Maltechnik.) München, 1897.

BORRADAILE, Rosamund and Viola, *Practical Tempera Painting: a student's 'Cennini'*. London, 1949.

BOLTZ, Valentinus, *Das Illuminierbuch: künstlich alle Farben zumachen und bereiten* [etc.]. Franfurt-am-Main, 1550. [Modern edition, edited by C. J. Benziger, Munich, 1913.]

CENNINI, Cennino, *[Il Libro dell'Arte.] A Treatise on Painting written* . . . *in the year* 1437 . . . Translated by Mrs. Merrifield. London, 1844.

———— *[Il Libro dell'Arte.] The Book of Art of Cennino Cennini* . . . Translated by Christiana J. Herringham. London, 1899.

———— *Il Libro dell'Arte.* Text edited by D. V. Thompson. (Italian & English.) 2 vols. New Haven, 1932, 1933.

DODOENS, Rembert, *A Nieuwe Herball, or Histories of Plantes* . . . *now first translated out of French into English* by H. Lyte. London, 1578 [and later editions].

EASTLAKE, Sir Charles L., *Materials for a History of Oil Painting*. 2 vols. London, 1841, 1869.

GERARDE, John, *The Herball, or generall Histories of Plantes*. London, 1597 [and later editions].

HILLIARD, Nicolas, *A Treatise concerning the Art of Limning*. (Edited by Philip Norman. Walpole Society, First Annual Volume.) London and Oxford, 1912.

HOLME, Randle, *The Academy of Armoury*. Vol. I. Chester, 1688. Vol. II. Edited by I. H. Jeayes. (Roxburghe Club.) London, 1905.

LYTE, Henry, see DODOENS.

MERRIFIELD, Mrs. Mary P., *The Art of Fresco Painting, as practised by the old Italian and Spanish Masters* . . . *With observations and notes*. London, 1846.

———— *Original Treatises dating from the XIIth to XVIIIth centuries on the Arts of Painting in Oil, Miniature, Mosaic and on Glass* [etc.]. 2 vols. London, 1849.

PACHECO, Francisco, *Arte de la Pintura*. Sevilla, 1649 [and later editions].

THEOPHILUS, *De diversis Artibus*. The various Arts. Translated from the Latin with introduction and notes by C. R. Dodwell. London, 1961.

THOMPSON, Daniel V., *[De Arte Illuminandi.] An anonymous fourteenth-century Treatise De Arte Illuminandi* . . . *Translated from the Latin* . . . by D. V. Thompson and G. H. Hamilton. New Haven, 1933.

———— *The Materials of medieval Painting*. London, 1936.

SOCIETY OF MURAL DECORATORS & PAINTERS IN TEMPERA. Papers. Vols. 1–4. London, 1924–1954.

INDEX

This index has been arranged with a view to enabling the reader to find with ease the more important processes described in the manuscript. It does not set out to give the number of every page on which reference is made to any given ingredient.

Alunen, 28–44
Andres von Colmar, 16, 26
Atrament, 40
Aurum Musitum, 26,94

Berger, Ernst, 4, 8, 88, 98, 100
Bermit (Pergament durchsichtig zu machen) 34, 64
Beins, gebrentes, 54, 60, 62
Bimses, 54
Bolum, Armenum, 64
Bol, Armenici, 60, 64
Boltz, Velentin, 88
Borradaile, V. & R., 104
Brisil Holtz, 22, 44
Brun Blau Tüchlin Varwe (Rezept), 30
Brun Rot, 56, 58

Cennini, Cennino, 10, 12, 70, 90, 106
Criden, 20, 24, 26

Eastlake, Sir Charles, 4, 8, 100, 106
Endich, 44, 54, 60, 102
Endich Grün, 54
Essich, 22, 28, 42, 52
Eyger Glor, 22, 24, 28, 90

Fundament (für Gold und Silber) 24, 26, 94

Alum (rock alum understood) in preparation of rag colours, 29–45
Andrew of Colmar, 17–27
Atramentum (for ink making), 41
Aurum musitum, 27, 95
Azurite, 47, 51, 55, 57, 59

Berger, Ernst, 5, 9, 89
Bilberries, 31, 41, 53
Bistre (refining of), 49, 55
Blue for missals, 39, 101
Bole, Armenian, 61, 65, 67
Boltz, Valentin, 89
Bone (calcined), 55, 61, 63
Borradaile, *Practical Tempera Painting,* 105
Brazil wood (preparation of rose pink), 23, 45

Cennini, Cennino, 11, 13, 71
Cinnabar, 91
Cinabrese, 91
Cornflowers (blue: receipt for making (blue 'rag colour'), 29, 31, 97
Cornflowers (pink: receipt for making violet 'rag colour'), 31
Cornflowers, dried (receipt for making a transparent blue glaze), 41
Colours for use with oil, 55

Deep blue 'rag colour' (receipt for making), 31

Eastlake, Sir Charles, 5, 9, 101, 107
Egg-yolk, 21, 23, 43

Flesh colour (how to mix), 57–59
Foundation (for gold and silver on parchment), 25, 27, 95

113

Glicen Steines, 54, 60, 64
Gallas Romanas, 40, 102
Gerarde, S., 98, 100, 102, 104, 110
Gold, 24, 26, 28, 60, 62
Gold Varwe (Rezept), 60, 64, 66
Gruner, Lewis, 8
Gumi Arab, 20, 50, 88
Gumi Cerusa, 42, 64
Gumi Amigdular, 64
Gumi Tragantum 46, 48, 52

Heidelber, 30, 40, 50, 52
Heinrich von Lübbegge, 14, 20
Honges, 24
Honges (also Bestandteil Gummi Bind-esmittels), 42
Honges (als Bestandteil Pergament Leims), 52

Kalk, 20, 44
Kornblumen (Blau), 28–30, 96
Kornblumen (Rot), 30
Kornblumen (getrocknet), 40

Lagga, 30, 98
Lazur, 20, 46, 50, 54, 56, 58
Libvarw, 56–58
Lin (oder Lim) Pergament, 52, 54, 104
Lampten, Lampeschen, 40, 42, 44, 98, 100, 102
Lougen, 20, 22, 44, 90
Lytes, Botany, 96, 100

Margasitan Argenteam, 26
Mastik, 36, 62, 66
Merrifield, Mrs. Mary, 12, 88, 94
Minium, 50–60, 64
Mirren, 28, 46

Gauze, 53, 109
Gerarde, S., 99, 101, 103
Gold (to lay on wood, etc.), 61, 63
Gold (for parchment), 25, 27
Gold (ground to a powder for working with), 29
Gold lacquer, 67
Gold size (receipt for making), 61, 65, 67
Glaire (how to make), 23, 25, 29, 91
Gruner, Lewis, 9
Gum, Arabic (in preparation of colours and mediums), 21–51, 89
Gum (of cherry tree), 43, 65
Gum (of almond tree), 65
Gum Lac, see Lac

Henry of Lubeck, 15, 21
Hilliard, The Whole Art of Limning, 89
Holmes, Armoury, 101
Honey (as ingredient of gum medium), 43
Honey (as ingredient of parchment size medium), 53
Honey (dry method of gilding on parchment), 25

Indigo (see also London indigo), 45, 55, 61, 103
Indigo Green, 55

Lac (see Paris Red), 99
Lead White, see White Lead
Lemnian earth, 25, 95
Lime, 21, 45
London, 39, 43, 45, 99, 101, 103
Lye, 21, 23, 45, 91
Lyte, Botany, 97, 101

Margasitan argenteam, 27
Mastic, 37, 63, 67
Merrifield, Mrs. Mary, 13, 89, 95
Mordant, see gold size
Myrrh, 29, 47

Naples Codex, 89, 97
National Gallery, London, 9

Oli (Hanfsamen), 54, 62
Oli (Linsamen), 54, 62, 106
Oli (Nuss), 54, 62
Oli (zum ferben), 52
Opiment, 22, 50, 54, 92

Oak apples (for making ink), 41, 103
Ochre, yellow (light and dark), 27, 55, 65, 109
Oil, hempseed (in varnish making), 55, 63
Oil, linseed (its preparation), 55
Oil, linseed (in varnish making) 63
Oil, walnut (for varnish making), 55, 63
Oil, spoonful of (for use in dyeing), 53
Orpiment, 23, 51, 55, 93

Pacheco, Francisco, 108
Paris, 40, 100
Paris Rot, 34, 48, 54, 56
Punicem Romanum, 28, 100

Pacheco, Francisco, 109
Parchment size *see* Size
Parchment (how to make it transparent), 35, 65,
Paris, 39, 101
Paris red (how to make and for shading), 35, 49
Pumice (use in sicatising oil), 55
Punicem Romanum, 29, 101

Roselin Varw, 32–34, 44, 50
Rus (Rezept), 48, 54
Ruschelecht, 54, 106

Realgar, 55, 107
Rag colours, 29, 31–33, 37, 39
Red lead, 51–61, 65
Rose colour, a transparent glaze from brazil wood (how to make), 33–35, 45, 51

Saffrans, 20, 24, 44, 90
Safft grün (Rezept), 48, 104
Salis Armoniac, 24, 32, 38, 40
Silber, 24, 26, 62, 66
Sinopia, 90
Spangrün, 20, 22, 36, 42, 54, 64
Stein, 60–62, 108
Substancie, 48, 104

Saffron, 21, 25, 45, 91
Sal ammoniac, 25, 33, 39–41
Sap green (how to make), 49, 105
Silver, 25, 27, 63, 67
Sinopia, 91
Size, parchment (how to make), 53, 105
Size, as medium for colours, 53–55
Stone, 61–63, 109

Theophilus, 10, 110
Thompson, D. V., 10, 88, 90, 92, 100
Tucklin Blau, 40, 100
Tudor-Hart, Percyval, 104, 106

Tartar (or tartarum, or Tartrate of Potash), 23, 43, 93
Tempera Society (formerly Society of Mural Decorators and Painters in Tempera), 3, 105
Terracotta, 61, 109
Theophilus, 71, 111
Thompson, D. V., 9, 89, 91, 93, 99, 101
Tile, 35, 99
Tragacanth, 47, 49, 53
Transparent colours, 43–53
Tudor-Hart, Percyval, 105, 107

Van Eyck, 14
Varwen (durschinigen), 42–52
Varwen (mit öli), 54
Varwen (Tuchlin), 28, 30, 32, 36, 38, 96
Verger/Steinverger, 26, 54–64, 108
Virnis (Verschiedene Rezepten), 54–66
Violvar Tuchlin (Rezept), 36
Vitrioli Iöni (ougstein), 40

Winstein, 22, 42, 92

Zendal, 52
Ziegel (Heidischen), 24, 94
Ziegelstein, 34, 98
Zinober, 20, 46, 56, 90

Van Eyck, 15
Varnish (how to make various kinds), 63–67
Varnish (ground into oil paints), 55
Varnish (for use of over size colours), 55
Varnish (as ingredient in gold lacquer laid over white metals), 67
Verdigris, 21, 23, 37, 43, 55
Verdigris (colour used for eyes), 65
Vermilion, 21, 47, 55, 91
Vinegar, 23, 43, 53, 65
Violet rag colour (how to make from poppies), 37
Vitriol of iron (for use in ink making), 41
Vitriol of zinc, 55, 61, 65

White lead, 45, 51, 55–61
White of egg *see* glaire
Whitsun and Whitsuntide, 29, 37, 97

Yellow, transparent glaze, 45–47